BIAFRA- ANCIENT IGBO LEADERSHIP STRUCTURE

-Pros & Cons of European Influence in Nigeria-

By Amaechi Obi

- Code for Human Unity, Peace & Harmony-

Table of Content

PREFACE

INTRODUCTION

PART 1

PART 2

PRO-INDEPENDENCE AND NIGERIAN LEADERS

PART 3

PART 7 - Prelude

PREFACE

This book is simply unique in every aspect. It contains authentic, simple and proven approach to achieve a realistic national and global unity, peace and harmony from the top to bottom! It is multi-faceted in its structure and presentation. The author ventured into most of the near forgotten history of the ancient Biafra who had been in existence between 400-500 BC; the era of the colonial pirates and their heinous amalgamation of the Hausas in the North, Yoruba's in the West and the Biafra's in the East and South which jointly gave birth to what we have today as 'Nigeria'. English language was imposed on the amalgamated Nigerians as to cap, curtail and belittle their ancestral heritage. Their genealogy, culture, history and human identity were duly desecrated, trampled upon and deeply hidden from the future generations; all to enhance and consolidate their elite agenda for political, economic and military domination. This very action obviously have near perpetually enslaved and impoverished the citizens who inhabit in those regions since from then to this present day.

'Nothing hidden under the sun that cannot be revealed with time'; nothing in this world remains the same with the passage of time; everything changes and are potentially made to change and not to remain static. On that note, it is obvious that time for change in ways of our global politics, economic dispensation, religious doctrine and lastly our collective education system; this is time to sit as brothers and sisters on a round table discussion and conscientiously unmake the mistakes from the past in order to enable this awesome world, full of awesome people to move further and farther forward under the umbrella of: unity, equality, peace and harmony!

The oil-boom from the seventies (1970) which lasted till nineteen-eighty-nine (1989) when the global economic policies swiftly hit the country below belt and knocked them out of the global strong economic arena. The purported oil boom opened ajar the gate of heart wrecking corruption, political mismanagement and manipulation of the highest order; and nepotism; these issues today are combining to give rise to mass youth agitation such as the Boko Haram which is busy unleashing the worst terrorism at all nook and cranny of Nigeria; indiscriminate multi-million Naira kidnap ransom demands; cult and ritual killings on a daily basis; the 'Niger Delta Avengers'; Bakassi; Massop; Arewa Youths; Oduduwa/Afanifere and the latest and most devastating, the IPOB founded by Nnamdi Kanu which is actually holding the amalgamated Nigeria in total ransom with demand for a referendum and for a peaceful separation of Biafra out of the amalgamated Nigeria; while many citizens in and out of the country press for a change of political status in the present to a more federal system where each region will be economically and politically autonomous from the incumbent unitary or unilateral system of government.

All these agitations and insurgencies are not just taking place in Nigeria alone; it is all taking place also across nations. And why is all that agitation and protests becoming more predominant in these recent years than ever in Nigeria?

Because the truth of the hidden evils orchestrated in the past are now surfacing gradually; the deceived and sleeping children are fast awakening; they are beginning to ask questions and without receiving cogent answers, and their anger is soaring as far as they continue to unveil the secret files revealing the past national and global mismanagement by the political elites who are keeping them and their pretty environment so impoverished and without any sign of near relief.

The time on the bomb is ticking! The secrets are now known and the game is over! We now need to sit back and rewrite the history of the world making honest effort to put everything back in their rightful perspective in order to minimize these rising level of human and environmental casualties within every nook and cranny. Time has come for amends, apologies, reunions and forgiveness as to pave way for brotherhood and sisterhood in all our neighborhoods!

We cannot continue to close our eyes on these pending challenges; another renaissance in the human history is what the world is undergoing without knowing it. In this indomitable global clamor for freedom, change, unity and equality, to fast-forward this ceaseless clamoring and natural desire for freedom and fairness, the sovereign nations of Asia, Africa and South America among others should lead the way by – carving out a good area of land in one of their best and secured areas, build a mega city which will be exclusively reserved for those of their distant brothers and sisters who were mistakenly taken as slaves in the past demonstration of human ignorance and heinous ingenuity. Those continents should begin to prepare a comfortable and ultra-modern city for those wishing to trace and come back to their roots could do so without bureaucratic impediments.

Another good thing the continents of Asia, Africa and South America in particular should do to push the process of unification, equality and change is – to construct another mega-city for thousands of their youths in prisons all over the world due to political instabilities and unemployment rampant in their countries of origin; and above all that, to reform their political and religious dogmas to allow more youth participation in the decision makers of their respective communities. The future belongs to the youths, so let them start to take their destinies in their hands as earlier as possible; desist from victimizing your growing youths for they are your security; they are your survivors and there is nothing anyone can do about certain things of creation order than facing up to them squarely.

Enough is enough, lets us start all over again as brothers and sisters and with unity and peace vision behind our minds. 'United we stand firm and secured, divided we weaken and continue to fall'.

If we cannot sit and correct these pending anomalies in our system of leadership, why then and with what audacity do we continue to preach unity or peace; form and fund organizations of diverse calibers entrusted with the holistic duty to establish unity, peace and equality while we all now know that we know the details of and causes of majority of the terrorism, religious extremism, economic and political sabotage… we cannot any more afford to pretend or remain ignorant of the obvious facts of our personal, national and international challenges.

This is a renaissance of a global dimension that extends beyond boarders; an urgent need to resolve all our challenges with frankness and humility; enough of keeping secrets for us; we have grown strong and matured enough to handle any kind of truth about our lives and our origin. Who are our forefathers, where did we come from, what are the truth about religion and its rise, what are the final agenda and mission of our leaders??? We are no more contented nor in agreement with the way in which, this awesome world is being continuously devastated regrettably by our kind of legislator upon whom we did entrusted with the sacred duty of its care and salvation, than from unknown wrongdoers! Nigeria, Biafra, Yoruba or Hausa agitations are only clamors for unity, freedom to live their God given lives in brotherhood and sisterhood in all their neighborhoods and I do not see anything wrong with fixing issues and mistakes for things to function smoothly in pace with peoples´ natural abilities.

Introduction

This book is based on the information gathered from peoples 'work, through the media network and my own personal experience as an Igbo origin. My birth came a couple of years after the Nigerian independence from the British colonial people therefore; there is no way I could write about the true history of either the Igbo/Biafra or Nigeria history out of my personal experiences or eyewitness.

The stories surrounding the true origin of the Igbo tribe, who their real ancestors were, is clouded in uncertainty. And that is due to the fact that there is no realistic written history or documented facts on the tribe of the Igbos or the defunct Biafra.

In this short book, I will write based on my childhood experiences, knowledge gathered from my autonomous community 'Ugbelle', where my grandfather, his father and ancestors in lineage grew and died. It will suffice also to know that my own grandfather lived a healthy 105 years in my autonomous community 'Ugbelle' before his death in 1986; and was over 80 years before my birth as one of his numerous grandchildren.

Like many, I was born as an Igbo origin and Nigerian by imposed nationality of which I know nothing about and of which, I have accepted my fate with pride and utmost patriotism without any reason whatsoever to think on the contrary. But, now as I sit writing, my faith and belief have been deeply shaken due to some information being spread around:

-How the Biafra map was deliberately deleted from the world map and replaced with that of Nigeria as we have it today.

-How the British colonialist with other European countries, out of selfish interest amalgamated or merged three whole ethic group of people and renamed them what we today call 'Nigeria' irrespective of their cultural, language and physical diversities and to crown it, imposed a foreign language and education on them; the reason why we all today speak English and very badly at the expense of our original and ancestrally inherited languages.

-This singular act of wicked amalgamation, without knowing it, is the main reason Nigerian people are unable to unite in peace and harmony; the main reason Nigerians being so highly intelligent and clever people are yet, unable to excel technologically and be self-sufficient; the main reason also, why you have the alarming high level of lack of patriotism and devastating corrupt practices helping in no small measure to strangulate the so called Nigeria!

-The main reason why people are also hungry in the means of abundance because none of the tribes feel they are living in their own country with their own ethic people; a uniform or common language is what nature had designed to classify people of the same genealogy or family tree; without that, anywhere you go, you are a foreigner because your language and cultural upbringing varies…you cannot toy with the forces of nature and have it your way; we are the created and not the Creator.

Without much preamble, I want to state categorically clear that the major contents in this book are excerpts from "National Code for Peace & Harmony" that very book was written early 2015 at the peak of political campaigns, elections and economic upheaval in Nigeria. As I write this, hundreds of copies of the said books are still waiting in the printer's storeroom for me to launch and present them to the general public so they can peruse and appreciate my creative genius…

The said book contains mostly universal principles of leadership structure which, I'm 100% faithful that shall not fail to bring and promote peace and harmony in any nation of this world, especially in the Biafra context if implemented with the right zeal and determination. "National Code for Peace & Harmony" was a compilation of my personal experiences as a humble child from a humble family in Imo State of formal Nigeria, (now confirmed Biafra land); who left home with all good intents and purposes out to the harsh world in personal search for truth, wisdom and the biblical promised land!

In those days, as I journeyed across horizons around the continents that make up our collective world, armed with my ancestral education and cultural background; my colonial indoctrination and education in Nigeria, I was consciously and unconsciously recording my thoughts, experiences, scenes and ways of other cultures as I meandered through the heartlands of the continents.

These blind adventures within our universe helped to open my eyes and ears to the great conspiracy in every nook and cranny of this awesome world perpetrated from top level by purported public servants; and the continuous contradiction between our hypocritical governments, my ancestral education and the universal natural rules and regulations are some of the daunting issues that kept me jolted and questioning ceaselessly the rationale in all the established global institutions. What were the main missions and visions of all the established institutions prior to their foundations?

My core aim is to see nations in: love, unity and harmony with each other as brothers and sisters. That laudable vision lead me to write the book "National Code for Peace & Harmony" Immediately after writing and had the book printed in Enugu, while I was busy organizing for the book launch and presentation in my home state, Imo or Abuja as our capital; Nnamdi Kanu, IPOB were busy on the other side awakening people about Biafra and their nearly forgotten origin; with the help of the social media such as YouTube in particular, I also started researching and following history; the truth that a nation called Biafra was once in the world map from the beginning and today does not appear anywhere in the global cartography of nations is utterly questionable…

This discovery for me was the down-point, the bottom-line…that was why the said book was not launched yet after these discoveries. The bedrock of the said book which, proposed an infallible leadership structure to make Nigeria great and habitable once again… had been shaken by that naked truth of conspiracy against the Igbo-Biafrans and there is no way I could henceforth defend the contents in the book anymore due to that devastating revelation of utter brutality and injustice ceaselessly being done against my innocent race. I was discouraged to launch the book I wrote in support of Nigeria unity by the knowledge of the conspiracy and the wickedness shown to the Igbos of Biafra particularly in Nigeria as a nation and the world at large!

For the above reasons, I have just decided to re-title the book for a more meaningful and realistic end: to make Biafra a model nation which shall be governed by the universal principles of love, peace & harmony. As you progress towards the middle you will read about the Blue Print for a proactive leadership structure. On that note, I hereby present to you the code of unity, love and progress for the imminent Igbo/Biafra System Structure!

PART 1

WHO ARE THE IGBO/BIAFRANS AND THEIR ORIGIN?

Go to this link for more info on Biafra- https://en.wikipedia.org/wiki/Biafra

This information is in Wikipedia.org

Historical maps -25 Provinces of Biafra-

Meaning of "Biafra" and location

Little is known about the literal meaning of the word Biafra. The word Biafra most likely derives from the subgroup Biafar or Biafad of the Tenda ethnic group who reside primarily in **Guinea-Bissau. Manuel Álvares** (1526–1583), a Portuguese Jesuit educator, in his work *Ethiopia Minor and a geographical account of the Province of Sierra Leone*, writes about the *"Biafar heathen"* in chapter 13 of the same book. The word Biafar thus appears to have been a common word in the Portuguese language back in the 16th century

Early modern maps of Africa from the 15th–19th centuries, drawn by European cartographers from accounts written by explorers and travellers, reveal some information about Biafra: The original word used by the European travellers was not *Biafra* but *Biafara, Biafar* and sometimes also *Biafares*.

The exact original region of Biafra is not restricted to Eastern Nigeria alone. According to the maps, the European travellers used the word *Biafara* to describe the entire region east of River Niger going down to the Mount Cameroon region, thus including Cameroon and a large area around Gabon. The Bight of Biafra lies in the present South-South Region of Nigeria and was renamed to Bight of Bonny by the Nigerian Government. The word *Biafara* also appears on maps from the 18th century in the area around Gambia.

Biafra was a country that existed on the Ancient Map of Africa for about 400 years before Nigeria was created by Captain Lugard and Rev. C.H. Robinson in 1914. In fact, by the year 1662, the three prominent Kingdoms in West Africa were the Kingdom of Biafra in the East, the Kingdom of Benin in the West and the Kingdom of Zamfara in the North. The country was then spelt as "Biafara". Here are some of the Ancient Maps of Africa showing the three Kingdoms. In 1884-1885, the Europeans and Americans met in the Berlin Conference, Germany, and spread the map of Africa on a table and shared the lands of Africa among themselves for colonization and exploitation of the resources of Africa. This is known in history as the Scramble for Africa. It was from these three kingdoms that Nigeria was created in 1914.

Biafra Maps With all these Ancient Africa maps showing us that Biafra Nation exist, why is it that all the modern maps of Africa try to exclude Biafra and other ancient nations alike?

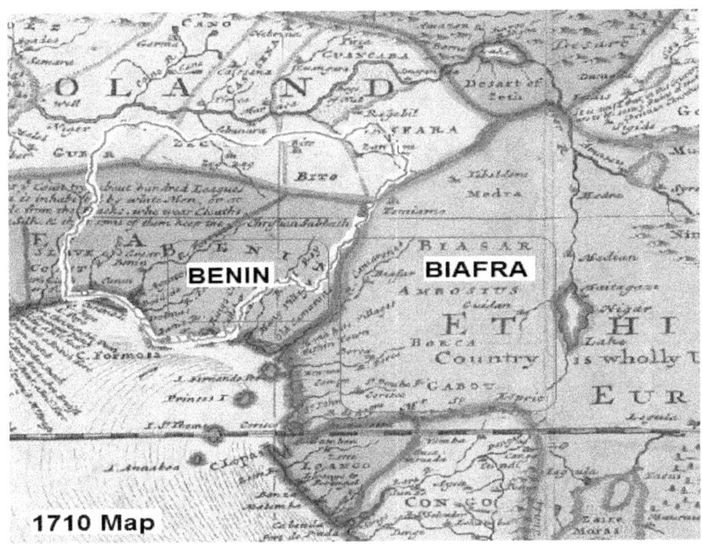

-**The ancient map of Africa in 1662 showed the three kingdoms in West Africa from where the new country called Nigeria was created.**

-Do you know that the **Ancient Map** of world of early 14 and 15th Century drawn by the cartographers has **Biafra** in it?

-There had been from **ancient map** bigger country named **Biafra** which covered the present day **Biafra** and parts of southern Cameroon.

IGBO-BIAFRA ETHNIC CULTURAL CONCEPT

From my point of view as an Igbo origin who lived for long outside of Nigeria and Biafraland; and with profound global experience and an extended view of this awesome world. My aim here is to categorically assert that the Igbos and most people originating from the East-Southern part of what we today know as Nigeria are people who are spiritually bound and linked to the unseen God or Chukwu Okike Abiama inherited from their ancestral culture, tradition and concept of life in general.

As a child, I was fortunate to be born under the umbrella of such ancestors with good record of long, healthy, happy and fruitful lives. In Ugbelle, my ancestral village, I was able to experience the brutal conflict between the Igbo ancestral customary structure and lifestyle which was anchored in awe, love and self-imposed loyalty to Chukwu Okike Abiama or God; with the contemporary system or human civilization which on the other hand is anchored in competition, negative exploration and exploitation of the binding forces of the Creator.

Discrimination, disrespect and wanton competition were nearly inexistent within the ancient structured hierarchy. Every inhabitant in this region was usually given effusive respect and accepted just as they are from birth without adding or subtracting. "Everything and every person is designed and created by Chukwu Okike Abiama; it is offensive and inappropriate to add, subtract or modify peoples' natural features in their view and concept of life in general except, of course, when Culture and the divine spirit/s demand of them to carry out such acts in conformity with the wishes and desires of Chukwu Okike Abiama; for example, their custom of circumcision and child-naming-ceremony.

Child-Naming: in Ugbelle as in other villages in Biafraland, giving name to a child is based on a kind of incarnation with the belief that, their dead and gone ancestors will always return to life through any child in Ugbelle especially, most related family members from the same village or ancestral lineage. Usually, the name of any of a dead relative is given by a special overseer or fortune-teller' to a new born child as a middle name and in that case, the child is said to be a reincarnation of...the basis and criterion for such communication with the dead and name giving is unclear and undisclosed to the public...in the same vein, circumcisions was and still is very actively adhered to among the Igbos but, the main reason behind this concept and culture for circumcising all male and female children are also undisclosed to the masses as in most things involving tradition and cultural knowledge in Igbo/Biafra

Igbo ancestors were kind of experts in instilling discipline, sense of auto esteem and a positive approach to work and life in general. They never tried to change or deeply interfere with the things of creation except in moments to express their sincere superstitious concepts. They took out of the land only what they require for food and sustenance. They criticize and condemn any wrong or negative use of lands and resources found in and within their given habitat. Unity, natural love, peace and harmony were the guiding and leading principles and objectives of all their promulgated rules and regulations which, customarily, bind and guide their people towards the path to goodness and positive deeds and thoughts!

Conflict of Culture and Concept

With time and progress, some of the best intrinsic values inherent among the Igbos were being entangled and corrupted with other norms and concepts of life from other cultural background. It was a very sad situation for the Igbo ancestors when they had to contend with the negative influences of the colonialists; who brought and imposed upon them, their own style of education, religious and administrative structure which today as I write, remain one of the worst act of evil done against the Igbos of Biafra, Africa in general and many other parts of this world. And, that bad influence is in all aspect weighing down the natural pace of rise and growth in the entire African continent without exception.

However, in my view, there is nothing wrong adopting and adapting to new concepts and perceptions for embracing things of nature in a different way and to blending the new with the old; *the present or new is always a vestige from the old and the past or old is the sum of the present*. Whatever experience we perceived in the course of our respective lives cannot simply be wiped away from us without our consent or collaboration. The easiest way to get people to forget and neglect what they have seen, known or possess is either through persuasion or coercion; but, humans mostly employ coercion and deceit more than persuasion.

The colonialists who invaded Africa many years ago had behind their minds the secret intention to divide and rule most of the countries, the hidden intention to infiltrate, adulterate and indoctrinate people in conceiving and perceiving spiritual and physical reality in their own image. This is the period of commencement of the timeless delusion and mental slavery of the Africans and of course, the world at large… this is from where the conflicts we are living today in Nigeria and Biafra started. As I write, most Igbo-Biafrans are paying huge prices from that conspiracy orchestrated long time ago by the colonialist and some dishonest Nigerians. The Igbo/Biafra customs and traditions were fully infiltrated, adulterated and the real truth deeply hidden from the growing youth and replaced instead, by mass negative indoctrination in the guise of mass education and religious fineness.

IGBO/BIAFRA RELIGION AND DIVINE CONCEPT

The world should know and take into consideration the obvious fact that ancient African people and their children were never taught in an established and institutionalized place of: worship, school of learning, ethics and work factories. Many of the African parents we see today are direct descendants of people who solely and solidly attached their live and beliefs in the sure hands of the Creator- God- Chineke…

The African ancestors had for millions of years lived in their natural habitats making their own rules and regulations, feeding, building and educating their own families with their unadulterated perception of all lives in this universe.

They never went to any kind of schools or churches and, therefore, could not read or write in any given language whatsoever. They communicate mostly through signs, gestures and practical deeds irrespective of their unwritten inherited local languages/vernaculars.

Most ancient African natives never practiced any written religion; they used carved figures or live-trees to represent their belief in a Supreme Being. They knew nothing about the bible, Quran or any other form of religious worship as we have in this present time. For such belief and concept they were classified as heretics – non believers; Idol worshippers by the modern civilization etc. *an ugly conspiracy*

A close observation, experiences and confessions from other people around the world as I sit writing today, reveals the obvious fact that 'the heaven should be for the Africans; the heaven should reserve a major portion of land for the Africans because they have lived all these millions of years in absolute peace and harmony with all things of creation and themselves. Because they lived with natural thought and perception of the world as they see and feel it without this modern greedy ambition to change most created things of God or Chineke. Because they lived, mingled and worked with animals, plants and other creatures without discrimination or the pseudo-superiority syndrome of the modern societies.

On a broader perspective, my grandfather and his era in majority were concrete examples of all I have said in favor or against our great ancestors; those people were naturally very religious in every sense of the terminology 'religious'. They understood and believed in Karma and Reincarnation and ultimately, in the unseen and most Supreme God/Chineke. They worshipped fervently and remained unshakably loyal, thankful and appreciative of good fortunes and in the same vein intolerant to whatever they considered immoral, bad and negative things or deeds; of which, they devised ways to sanitize their every ill or misfortune through giving a corpus material objects – offering- in the witness of a carved image or living tree which, shall intercede or intervene between their misfortune and 'Chineke'- the 'Supreme and unseen Creator' for respite, forgiveness and remedy. In the same way they offer sacrifices to God through small gods for thanksgiving and show of gratitude!

As far as history and experience show, the Igbos of Biafra are very highly religious; so religious and faithful to the unseen Creator, so much so that, nearly every given name in Igbo have some message of praise or assertion of their proud proclamation of the Unseen Creator; for example: Chineke- 'God the Creator'

Chukwudi- 'There is God'

Ekeledirichukwu- Thanks be to God; glory to God'

Chikaodinaka- in God's hands' etc.

The Igbo in Biafraland have Chineke or Chukwu Okike Abiama – God- as their guiding father in spiritual and physical dimensions. The Igbo ancestors from the start somehow believed so much in the unseen creator that, they deeply accepted the naked fact that without trust and belief in God, nothing worthwhile can be achieved. They fear shedding of human blood unless under extreme cultural or natural coercion. They believed also in Karma and Reincarnation; from such belief, they designed a way of life deeply entrenched in love, appreciation, compassion, peace and unity with their people and environment ever in consciousness that whatever wrong one does against the gods' must be penalized in the next life, for that, they shun evil acts and strive to do just what they perceived as good deeds!

The Igbo of Biafra originally were just easy-going, natural and God fearing people. Today, as I write, the cultural beliefs, tradition and system structure of the Biafra Igbo are being gradually polluted, discredited through some classified and secret political agendas from the top to down.

The above negative political and religious conspiracies from higher places are the root cause why the Igbos of Biafra is scattered and found all over the world in desperate search for self identity and livelihood. The end of the 6th of July 1967 – 15th of January 1970 Nigeria/Biafra war paved the way for a massive national indoctrination program in the guise for good education and the promise of a brighter and better future which obviously was the opposite to the truth before all of us today. Before these periods, the Igbos of Biafra naturally loved themselves so much they hardly marry outside of their respective clans and ethnic groups. Their only and major worry at the time to contract marriage vows was to not marry someone from the same immediate family lineage. They believed that it is contra-productive to contract a marital relationship with same family blood or bear children together. A background inquiry on the intending marriage couples are usually carried out in order to ascertain there were no ancestral blood mixture between the prospective marrying couple before they shall be legally endorsed to tango in respect to their well structured community rules and regulations.

The Igbos of Biafra and basically, the rest of African nations were duly lead and governed in the past before colonialism through an innate democratic community structure usually based on self and community sustenance; backed by individual determination and perseverance against all human and natural challenges to life and progress.

Cultural Background & System Structure-

In the ancestral Igbo-Biafran political system structure, natural wisdom and individual strength was the major determinant factor for electing and endorsing: Clan, kindred and community leaders. Then, that trait is followed by individual attitude and concept in the general structure of this universe as perceived and conceived. Buying and selling with money was never part of their major agendas towards life at larger extent. They fully embraced the positive spirit of sharing and giving out their entire material surpluses to immediate relations, neighbors, friends and community development. They were right to believe that 'Chineke – God- owns and gives all; and nothing is truly theirs. They never practiced hoarding of information, wealth and resources as being done in this present era.

CONTEMPORARY BIAFRAN YOUTH *-Igbos in Particular-*

Let it clearly be stated here now that, the major issues and challenges in this moment for the Biafra-Igbos is not just to struggle to achieve independence or sovereign nation for themselves. The major and most fundamental vision and mission should be to achieve this long awaited Biafra restoration of independence with the deepest Godly intentions to make of Biafra a model nation worthy of emulation; not only in a measure of material and technological prowess but, to also strive against all obvious odds to structure Biafraland and citizens as models and harbingers of resilient moral rectitude, such as seen during the era of the great Igbo/Biafran ancestors when, mere spoken words were considered as good and binding as any form of signed agreement in this current era; when the Igbos and other ethnic groups lived in communities as families sharing, helping and eating with each other in absolute and natural unity, peace and harmony.

-To make Biafra or any other nation united in peace and harmony, you cannot reject, neglect and abandon your inherited tree of life or lineage; your human origin. In human life, as an intrinsic law, one can only succeed and progress faster nearly in every life's facet by incorporating and embracing your ancestral legacies; modify, rectify and carry the concept to the next level of advancement; focusing on the gradual alleviation and not enhancing your collective challenges or problems…without such mindset in the founding fathers of a family or nation, long-term success and unity will hardly foster.

-Any man-made rules, old or new that are not helping the people in a positive and harmonious ways should duly be deleted and replaced with rules and regulations which will benefit and enhance people progress generation after generation.

Why am I saying these things?

Stop, ponder and take a brief analysis of a nation like Nigeria and citizens for example; starting from the 1960 independence till today- 27th of May 2017- how many decades of self-rule have transpired? What is your personal observation and opinion? In my view, after six (6) decades of sovereignty, Nigeria as a nation is still enmeshed in the worst political irresponsibility ever seen anywhere in the present modern world; outright lack of patriotism, awful, belittling and shameful corrupt practices; open and proud manifestation of wickedness. Aimless and hopeless ambition from top down; dark and slimy occult practices from top down, kidnapping, bribery, human and organ trafficking, appropriation and embezzlement of public funds.

On the other side, the most lucrative scam from the churches in the name of our venerated Creator- ′Chukwu Okike Abiama-God all Mighty′ coupled with unreligious/religious fanaticism and terrorism secretly coordinated by people in higher places hiding under the umbrella of political immunity. In a nutshell, the country Nigeria' from the onset is a sale-out. Nigeria is like a country under some kind of negative spiritual bondage; a nation without a clear goal for unity, peace and balanced progress. A nation bound and stagnant under archaic and unfruitful religious, ethnic and cultural beliefs and practices…

In the context of the imminent Biafra independence, notwithstanding, the relevant point here is that, up until this few years, we have all been fed and educated, indoctrinated and partially or fully influenced by the negative vices stated above which are the nucleus of ceaseless agitations and revolt ever since Nigeria independence; which is rendering the nation more ungovernable day after day. To separate Biafra from Nigeria without separating the negative influences acquired through education, and the negative mental attitude trending in the country as I sit writing, Biafra as a nation when achieved, run and governed by men and women imbibed with the same mindset or mental attitude rooted in inhuman vices, mischief and unpatriotic tendencies, Biafra will not go far in that kind of poor mindset! And even if Biafra sustained for long in such poor and low human attitude, strife, open and proud wickedness shall be the commonest scenario.

Despite the Nigeria education and bad influences duly acquired so far, most of the inherited and ancestral legacies to the Igbo people in the areas of custom and tradition on themselves; do not make the Igbo/biafrans the best and ideal humans either. Therefore, for Biafrans to make a difference and correct the vices inherited from Nigeria, their ancestors and triumph as a model nation worthy to emulate in terms of Godly unity, peace and harmony amongst them as in the era of their great ancestors, they must structure and build in the similar outlook and mindset of their ancestors – 'selflessly'! Having said this, I feel obliged to elucidate and to make my views clearer with the following guidelines based on Natural or Godly principles for a harmonious lifestyle.

To make a difference in others you must start within yourself to discover how to change you first; the good change occurring in you will naturally attract and absorb others and, ultimately, communities and nations shall change in a natural gradual process without arms or coercion!

PART 2

PRO-INDEPENDENCE NIGERIANS AND LEADERS

Nnamdi Azikiwe - *Journalist, political activist*

Playing a key role in Nigeria's emergence as a free nation, Nnamdi Azikiwe served as the first president of Nigeria after it was given independence from Great_Britain in 1960. Much of his life was spent working as both a journalist and politician to end British control of Nigeria. Known widely as "Zik of Africa," Azikiwe was also a mentor to Kwame Nkrumah, who as president of Ghana became head of the first African country to free itself from European rule.

As was written in an obituary in a 1996 issue of *Jet*, "Known as a vigorous champion of African independence from European colonial rule, Dr. Azikiwe attained the rare status of national hero, admired across the regional and ethnic lines dividing his country." For much of his life Azikiwe was a staunch defender of his Ibo people, and he helped to end the Biafran civil war that oppressed his tribe in the late 1960s. He was known as a charismatic orator who could sway large crowds with his emphatic delivery, and he frequently traveled to other countries to promote his causes.

Born in northern Nigeria in 1904, Azikiwe was the son of a member of the Ibo tribe who worked for the government. His early schooling was at the English-run Church Missionary Society's Central School at Onitsha and the Hope Waddel Training Institute at Calabar. After Azikiwe graduated from the Methodist Boys' High School in Lagos at the top of his class in 1925, his father granted him some funds so that he could travel to the United_States and further his education.

Azikiwe's American studies began at Howard University, where he played soccer and was taught by Ralph Bunche, who later achieved fame as a diplomat. He also studied at Storer College in West_Virginia, Lincoln University in Pennsylvania, and Columbia University in New York City while in the United States. After receiving his B.A. degree in 1930 from Lincoln University, Azikiwe stayed on for two years as an instructor and to pursue undergraduate work. He cut his teeth as a journalist during summer jobs as a reporter with the Baltimore *Afro-American*, Philadelphia *Tribune*, and the Associated Negro Press in Chicago.

In 1934 he returned to Africa after five years in the United States and made his debut as a journalist there, becoming editor-in-chief of the *African Morning Post*.

Born Benjamin Azikiwe on November 16, 1904, in Zungeru, Nigeria; died 1996; married Flora Ogbenyeanu Ogoegbunam, 1936; children: three sons, one daughter. *Education:* Lincoln University, B.A, 1930; University of Pennsylvania, M.A. Attended Howard University and Columbia University;

Became first Nigerian to study in United States, 1925; served as instructor at Lincoln University, 1931-34; became editor of *African Morning Post*, Ghana, 1934; founded *West African Pilot*, Nigeria, 1937; helped found National Council of Nigeria and the Cameroons (NCNC), 1944; served as president of NCNC, 1946-60; became member of Nigerian legislative council, 1947; elected to Eastern Region Assembly of Nigeria, 1953; became premier of the Eastern Region Assembly, 1954; became president of the Nigerian senate, 1959; became governor-general of Nigeria, 1960; served as president of Nigerian republic, 1963-66.

Selected awards: Nnamdi Azikiwe Distinguished Endowed Chair in International Relations, Lincoln University.

In Accra, Gold Coast (which later became Ghana). Three years later he started up the *West African Pilot* in Lagos, Nigeria, then built his newspaper holdings to including four other city newspapers. Azikiwe used his various publications to actively promote nationalist fervor and attack racial prejudice in the African colonies.

Political Prominence Grew

Starting in the mid 1940s, Azikiwe pressed his cause for Nigerian autonomy on the political front as well. He played a key role in the founding of the National Council of Nigeria and the Cameroons (NCNC) in 1944, becoming its first secretary general and then its president in 1946. The prominence of the NCNC and the Ibo people grew under Azikiwe's leadership. He used the NCNC to push for various reforms, including universal adult suffrage, direct elections, control of the civil service by African ministers, and Nigerian control of the territory's armed forces. Azikiwe became more of a thorn in the side of the status quo in 1947 when he became a member of the legislative council in Nigeria. In this position he strove to improve conditions for his people via changes in the constitution. During a 1947 visit to England, he told the British that big problems would result if Nigeria was not granted freedom in 15 years, according to an article in the *New York Herald Tribune*.

After a new constitution for Nigeria was drafted in 1951, the interests of the three regions of the country took precedence over the interest of the whole country. Azikiwe maintained a political balancing act during this period in order to maintain his power. By 1952 he had become the first NCNC opposition leader in the Western House of Assembly, then he was elected to the eastern region assembly in 1953. In the summer of that year, he traveled to London with a Nigerian delegation and demanded that Nigeria become self-governing within three years. Disputes arose over Britain's demand to separate Lagos, which was Nigeria's capital and chief port, from the western region. Further discussions were held among the various parties in Lagos in early 1954, at which time it was agreed that a more conclusive conference on Nigeria's future would be conducted in 1956.

Building his power in the Eastern Region, Azikiwe became its premier in 1954 after a new constitution was put into effect. He instituted a new education program in his region, and had a major role in Nigeria becoming the leading exporter of students for study abroad in Africa. In 1954 Azikiwe visited Europe, England, the United States, and Canada with members of the Eastern region economic commission in order to promote investment for developments in textile, vegetable oil refineries, steel, and chemicals.

Azikiwe had extensive business interests that brought him a significant income during the 1950s. He was assailed with allegations of corruption from other leaders in the mid 1950s, accused of having withdrawn $5.6 million in government funds and depositing it in a bank of which he was a shareholder to prevent the bank's collapse, according to a 1956 article in *Time* magazine. Despite being found guilty of improper conduct by a British tribunal in 1957, Azikiwe was still reelected as premier when he dissolved his legislature under pressure and called for a new election in 1956. "When, five years before independence, Azikiwe was exposed as having used his political position to further his financial interests through the African Continental Bank, he still retained the support the Ibo in the Eastern Region; for they believed that he was working for them and so entitled to become wealthy," noted John Hatch in *Africa Emergent*.

Azikiwe's political stance at this time clearly favored his Ibo tribe and the Ibibio-speaking peoples of the Eastern region. After Obafemi Awolowo, an enemy of Azikiwe, formed the Action Group in the West, Azikiwe aligned himself with Abubakar Tafaw Balewa, who had gained control of the Northern People's Congress. Since the Northern Region was most populous and had a political stance more acceptable to the withdrawing British, Balewa began to lead a new national regime in 1957. Azikiwe's alliance with Balewa helped him be named president of the senate in 1959, then governor-general.

When Nigeria's first independent government was established by a coalition of northern and eastern political parties in 1960, Azikiwe was named president and Balewa became prime minister. While new elections in 1964 kept Azikiwe in office, political instability led to agitation throughout the country. In January of 1966, a military coup d'état ousted Azikiwe from power. After Biafra tried to secede from Nigeria in 1967 and created a civil war in the country, Azikiwe backed his fellow Ibo and traveled widely in other

African nations to seek recognition of Biafra as an independent nation. Then he incurred the wrath of his former supporters in 1969 when he began backing the federal government in the war. In the years following the war, Azikiwe became a key opponent of the ruling party. Following the creation of a new constitution in Nigeria in 1978 that ended a 12-year ban on political parties, he ran as a candidate for the new Nigerian People's Party but was defeated.

Throughout his career, Azikiwe used his nationalist press, political connections, and kinship of his tribe to promote education, self-government, welfare, and progress. He also wrote over a dozen books on the struggle for African nationalism and other topics. He died in 1996 after a long illness, at the age of 91.

Major General Johnson Thomas Umunnakwe Aguiyi-Ironsi

Was born 3 March 1924 in Umuahia – died on 29 July 1966, Lalupon, Oyo State; a Nigerian soldier. He served as the Head of State of Nigeria from 16 January 1966 until he was overthrown and killed on 29 July 1966 by a group of northern army officers who revolted against the government.

Thomas Umunnakwe Aguiyi-Ironsi was born to Mazi Ezeugo Aguiyi's on 3 March 1924, in Umuahia-Ibeku, present-day Abia State, Nigeria. When he was eight years old, Ironsi moved in with his older sister Anyamma, who was married to Theophilius Johnson, a Sierra Leonean diplomat in Umuahia. Ironsi subsequently took the last name of his brother-in-law, who became his father figure. At the age of 18, Ironsi joined the Nigerian Army against the wishes of his sister.

Aguiyi-Ironsi enlisted into the Nigerian Army on 2 February 1942 and was admitted and excelled in military training at Eaton Hall, England and also attended Royal Army Ordnance Corps before he was later commissioned officer as an infantry officer in the rank of Lieutenant on 12 June 1949. He soon returned to Nigeria to serve as the aide-de-camp to John Macpherson, Governor General of Nigeria and he was assigned as equerry to Queen Elizabeth II during her visit to Nigeria in 1956, for which assignment he was sent to Buckingham Palace to train.

During the Congo Crisis of the 1960s, the United Nations Secretary-General, Dag Hammarskjöld, appealed to the Nigerian government to send troops to Congo. Lieutenant Colonel Ironsi led the 5th battalion to the Kivu and Leopoldville provinces of Congo. His unit proved integral to the peacekeeping effort, and he was soon appointed the Force Commander of the United Nations Operation in the Congo.

In 1960 he led the Nigerian contingent in Congo. There he single-handedly negotiated the release of Austrian medical personnel and Nigerian troops when they were ambushed by Katangese rebels. For this he was awarded the 1st class Ritta Kreuz Award. He also single-handedly confronted an angry mob in Leopoldville, disbanding them. This and many other exploits earned him the name "Johnny Ironside", a corruption of his name "Ironsi" with reference to various British military historical parallels.

Ironsi returned from Congo in 1964 during the post-independence "Nigerianization" of the country's institutions of government. It was decided that the British General Officer Commanding (GOC) of the Nigerian Army, Major General Welby-Everard, would step down to allow the government to appoint an indigenous GOC. Ironsi led the pack of candidates jostling for the coveted position. A consensus was reached by the ruling Northern People's Congress (NPC) and National Council of Nigerian Citizens (NCNC) coalition government, and Ironsi became General Officer Commanding of the Nigerian Army on 9 February 1965.

The political crisis in post-colonial Nigeria precipitated into a breakdown of law and order in some of the country's provinces. The inability of Prime Minister Tafawa Balewa to quell the situation incited the military to terminate civilian rule in a bloody coup d'etat on 14 January 1966. The revolutionary soldiers, led by Major Chukwuma Kaduna Nzeogwu, an Igbo from Okpanam near Asaba, present day Delta state, eradicated the uppermost echelon of politicians from the Northern and Western provinces.

Though Ironsi, an Igbo, was originally slated for assassination, he was able to outmanoeuvre the rebellious soldiers in Lagos, the Federal Capital Territory. With President Nnamdi Azikiwe undergoing medical treatment in London, the surviving members of Balewa's cabinet resigned and handed Aguiyi-Ironsi the reins of power. Aguiyi-Ironsi then forced Senate president Nwafor Orizu, who was serving as acting president in Azikiwe's absence, to officially surrender power to him, ending the First Nigerian Republic.

Ironsi inherited a Nigeria deeply fractured by its ethnic and religious cleavages. The fact that none of the high-profile victims of the 1966 coup were of Igbo extraction, and also that the main beneficiaries of the coup were Igbo, led the Northern part of the country to believe that it was an Igbo conspiracy. Though Ironsi moved swiftly to dispel this notion by courting the aggrieved ethnic groups through political appointments and patronage, his failure to punish the coup plotters and the promulgation of the now infamous "Decree No. 34"—which abrogated the country's federal structure in exchange for a unitary one— crystallized this conspiracy theory.

During his short regime Aguiyi-Ironsi promulgated a raft of decrees. Among them were the Constitution Suspension and Amendment Decree No.1, which suspended most articles of the Constitution (though he left intact those sections of the constitution that dealt with fundamental human rights, freedom of expression and conscience was left intact). The Circulation of Newspaper Decree No.2 which removed the restrictions on press freedom put in place by the preceding civilian administration. According to Ndayo Uko, the Decree no.2 was to serve "as a kind gesture to the press.." to safeguard himself when he went on later to promulgate the Defamatory and Offensive Decree No.44 of 1966 which made it an "offense to display or pass on pictorial representation, sing songs, or play instruments the words of which are likely to provoke any section of the country."

The controversial Unification Decree No. 34 aimed to unify Nigeria into a unitary state. Even though this decree was abolished when Aguiyi-Ironsi was deposed and killed, the decree was to affect the Nigerian foreign policy decision making system in a significant way: the abolition of "independence" of the regions in foreign policy. Until then the

Nigerian regional governments could make their own foreign policies independent of the federal government. This decree removed Nigeria's many contradictory tunes on foreign policy and various "mini-embassies" abroad were closed down.

On July 29, 1966, Ironsi spent the night at the Government House Ibadan as part of a nation-wide tour. His host, Lieutenant Colonel Adekunle Fajuyi, Military Governor of Western Nigeria, alerted him to a possible mutiny within the army. Ironsi desperately tried to contact his Army Chief of Staff, Yakubu Gowon, but he was unreachable. In the early hours of the morning, the Government House, Ibadan, was surrounded by soldiers led by Theophilus Danjuma.

Danjuma arrested Ironsi and questioned him about his alleged complicity in the coup, which saw the demise of the Sardauna of Sokoto, Ahmadu Bello. Although some have argued that Fajuyi was not a target in this counter-coup, Theophilus Danjuma, William Walbe and others have gone on record to say that they probably wanted him "for questioning" as much as they did his boss, Aguiyi-Ironsi. Fajuyi was seen as a so-called progressive, who had supported the Nzeogwu coup in January of that year. The bullet-riddled bodies of Ironsi and Fajuyi were later found in a nearby forest, and Yakubu Gowon became the new Military Head of State.

Alhaji Sir Abubakar Tafawa Balewa, KBE(1) (December 1912 – January 15, 1966)

Was a Nigerian politician, and the only prime minister of an independent Nigeria. Originally a trained teacher, he became a vocal leader for Northern interest as one of the few educated Nigerians of his time. He was also an international statesman, widely respected across the African continent as one of the leaders who encouraged the formation of the Organization of African Unity (OAU). Nicknamed the Golden Voice of Africa because of his oratory, he stands one of the only three National Heroes of the Nigerian Nation.

Early life and career

In contrast with the largely aristocratic ruling elite in the north, many of whose ancestry derives from royal lineage, Balewa had very humble origins. His father was a slave who rose in service of the Madaki of Bauchi and became a district head.

According to family oral history, Balewa's paternal grandfather Isa was murdered in front of his family by his rival's agents. Isa's widow then took her infant son to Bauchi, where the Madaki of Bauchi took her in. Abubakar was born in December 1912 in the village of Tafawa Balewa, in modern day Bauchi state. He was his father's only child. The name of his birthplace was appended to Abubakar's name (Abubakar Tafawa Balewa). Tafawa Balewa village takes its name from two corrupted Fulani words: "Tafari" (rock) and Baleri (black). This may have contributed to the "Black Rock" nickname he acquired in later life. Although it is widely (incorrectly) presumed that he was Hausa, Balewa's father Yakubu Dan Zala was in fact of Bageri ethnicity, and his mother Fatima Inna was Fulani.

Education

He attended Quaranic school and learnt the first chapter of the Qur'an by heart. For his Western education he attended Bauchi Provincial School. According to his teacher and classmates he was a shy, quiet and not outstanding student. Although reserved by nature, he did commit a disciplinary infraction when he was caught outside school without permission, and smoking with his friends to boot. He was whipped as punishment. One of his juniors at school was Nuhu Bamalli (later

Foreign Minister). He later attended Katsina Teacher Training College (1928-1933) and grad
with a third class certificate. His best subject was unsurprisingly, English. He became a teache
irritated by a friend's remark that no Northerner had ever passed the exam for a Senior Teac
Certificate, Balewa duly sat the exam, and obtained the Certificate. He became headmaster c
Bauchi Middle School. He reported that the first white woman he ever set eyes on was I
Margery Perham (a renowned academic on African affairs) when she visited Nigeria c
investigation of native administration.

In 1945 he and other northerners (including Aminu Kano) obtained a scholarship to study a
University of London's Institute of Education (1945-1946), where he received a teac
certificate in history. When he returned to Nigeria he said he now saw the world with "new e
Balewa said he:

*"returned to Nigeria with new eyes, because I had seen people who lived without fear, who ob
the law as part of their nature, who knew individual liberty"*

He returned to Nigeria as a Native Authority Education Officer.

He was elected in 1946, to the colony's Northern House of Assembly, and to the Legis
Assembly in 1947. As a legislator, he was a vocal advocate of the rights of northern Nigeria
together with Alhaji Ahmadu Bello, who held the hereditary title of *Sardauna* of Sokotc
founded the Northern People's Congress (NPC).

Politics

Balewa was no firebrand political radical. He may have remained a teacher for the rest of his
had southern politicians such as the flamboyant intellectual Nnamdi Azikiwe not pushed
Nigerian independence. Although not overtly political he founded an organisation named
"Bauchi Discussion Circle" in 1943, and was elected vice president of the Northern Teacl
Association (the first trade union in Northern Nigeria) in 1948. Anxious not to be politi
upstaged by the southerners, Northern leaders sought educated Northerners to serve in poli
posts. Balewa helped found the Northern People's Congress (NPC), which was originally inter
as a cultural organisation but by 1951 morphed into a political party due to the need to prese
Northern response to the rapid and sophisticated political groupings emerging in the so
Balewa was called into political service as the Bauchi Native Authority's representative to
Northern House of Assembly. The House of Assembly also selected him to become a membe
the Nigerian Legislative Council.

Despite political involvement, Balewa remained suspicious of Nigerian unification and feared
the Northern Region would be dominated by the better educated and dynamic south. He said
"the southern tribes who are now pouring into the north in ever increasing numbers…do not
with the northern people in social matters and we…look upon them as invaders. Since 191
Brirish government has been trying to make Nigeria into one country, but the Nigerian pe
themselves are historically different in their backgrounds, in their religious beliefs and customs
do not show themselves any sign of willingness to unite. So what it comes to is that Nigerian

is only a British intention in the country."

Balewa administration

Balewa entered the government in 1952 as Minister of Works, and later served as Minister of Transport. In 1957, he was elected Chief Minister, forming a coalition government between the NPC and the National Council of Nigeria and the Cameroons (NCNC), led by Nnamdi Azikiwe. He retained the post as Prime Minister when Nigeria gained independence in 1960, and was reelected in 1964.

Prior to Nigeria's independence, a constitutional conference in 1954 had adopted a regional political framework for the country, with all regions given a considerable amount ofpolitical freedom. The three regions then were composed of diverse cultural groups. The premiers and some prominent leaders of the regions later took on a policy of guiding their regions against political encroachment from other regional leaders. Later on, this political environment influenced the Balewa administration. His term in office was turbulent, with regional factionalism constantly threatening his government.

However, as Prime Minister of Nigeria, he played important roles in the continent's formative indigenous rule. He was an important leader in the formation of the Organization of African Unity and creating a cooperative relationship with French speaking African Countries. He was also instrumental in negotiations between Moise Tshombe and the Congolese authorities during the Congo Crisis of 1960–1964. He led a vocal protest against the Sharpeville Massacre of 1960 and also entered into an alliance with Commonwealth ministers who wanted South Africa to leave the Commonwealth in 1961. However, a treason charge and conviction against one of the western region's leaders, Obafemi Awolowo, led to protest and condemnation from many of his supporters. The 1965 election in the region later produced violent protests. Rioting and violence were soon synchronous with what was perceived as inordinate political encroachment and an over-exuberant election outcome for Awolowo's western opponents.

As Prime Minister of Nigeria, Sir Abubakar Tafawa Balewa, from 1960 to 1961, doubled as Foreign Affairs advocate of Nigeria. In 1961, the Balewa government created an official Foreign Affairs and Commonwealth Relations ministerial position in favour of Jaja Wachuku who became, from 1961 to 1965, the First substantive Nigerian Minister of Foreign Affairs and Commonwealth Relations, later called External Affairs.

In 1963 he gave a spellbinding eloquent speech at the Addis Ababa (Ethiopia) inaugural conference of the Organisation of African Unity. As Prime Minister he maintained a thoroughly dignified comportment. A British acquaintance called him "perhaps the perfect Victorian gentleman". He gained several awards from the British: OBE in 1952, CBE in 1955, Knighted by Queen Elizabeth II in January 1960 and was awarded an honorary degree by the University of Sheffield in May 1960.

Balewa proposed an amendment to Nigeria's constitution to give due recognition to the nation building role played by then Governor-General Dr. Nnamdi Azikiwe. Balewa proposed that

"Nnamdi Azikiwe shall be deemed to have been elected President and Commander in-Chief of
Armed Forces" because "Nigeria can never adequately reward Dr. Azikiwe" for the nationalist
he played in building Nigeria and achieving independence. Azikiwe is referred to by name
Nigeria's 1963 constitution, and to my knowledge Azikiwe was the only living indivi
constitutionally enshrined by name in his democratic country's constitution.

Honors

In January 1960, Balewa was knighted by Elizabeth II as a Knight Commander of the Order of
British Empire. He was awarded an honorary doctorate from the University of Sheffield in M
1960.

Overthrow

On January 15, 1966 he was kidnapped from his official residence by armed soldiers who w
executing Nigeria's first military coup. He was missing for several days and a search for him
ordered by the new military regime headed by Major-General Aguiyi-Ironsi. His family and frie
continued to believe he was alive. Rumours claimed the rebel soldiers were holding him alive
that he would be released as part of a prisoner swap involving the imprisoned Chief Awolo
However these hopes were dashed when his decomposing corpse was found a few days la
dumped in a roadside bush. His corpse was taken to Ikeja airport in the company of Po
Commissioner Hamman Maiduguri, Inspector-General of Police Kam Selem, Maitama Sule and
wives Laraba and Jummai who accompanied it as it was flown to Bauchi where he was buried.
body now lies inside a tomb declared a national monument. The tomb includes a library an
mosque. The famous race course square in Lagos was renamed "Tafawa Balewa Square" in
memory. His image appears on the 5 Naira note.The Abubakar Tafawa Bal
University in Bauchi is named in his honour.

Chief Obafemi Awolowo or **Awo**

Chief Obafemi Awolowo or **Awo** (born March 6, 1909, Ikenne, Colony and Protectorate of Southern Nigeria—died May 9, 1987, Ikenne, Nigeria), Nigerian statesman who was a strong and influential advocate of independence, nationalism, and federalism. He was also known for his progressive views concerning social welfare.

Awolowo was born in Ikenne, then part of the British Colony and Protectorate of Southern Nigeria. The son of a peasant, Awolowo first studied to be a teacher and later worked as a clerk, trader, and newspaper reporter while organizing trade unions and participating in nationalist politics in his spare time. In the 1930s he became an active member of the Lagos Youth Movement—later the Nigerian Youth Movement—and rose to become its secretary for the Western Province. During that time he came to bemoan the ethnic divisions within the nationalist movement and the growing political inequalities between some of Nigeria's ethnic nationalities and regions.

Awolowo went to London in 1944 to study law, and while there he founded the Egbe Omo Oduduwa (Yoruba: "Society of the Descendants of Oduduwa") to promote the culture and unity of the Yoruba people, one of the three largest ethnic groups in colonial Nigeria, and to ensure a secure future for them. During that period Awolowo also wrote the influential *Path to Nigerian Freedom* (1947), in which he made his case for the need of a federal form of government in an independent Nigeria to safeguard the interests of each ethnic nationality and region and to create a sustainable basis for Nigerian unity. He also called for rapid progress toward self-government.

In 1947 Awolowo returned to Ibadan to practice law, and the following year he established the Egbe Omo Oduduwa in Nigeria. In 1950–51 he founded a political party, the Action Group, with some of the Egbe's members as its nucleus, and in the process became the party's first president. The party called for an immediate end to British rule and for the development of several social welfare programs. In 1951 the party won the first elections held in the Western Region, one of the colony's three administrative divisions, and Awolowo later served as leader of government business and minister for local government structure, the latter for which he established elective councils. From 1954 to 1959, as premier of the Western Region, Awolowo worked to improve education, social services, and agricultural practices, implementing many progressive policies. Notably, his administration introduced programs that provided free health care for children and free universal primary education. The first television station in Africa was established in the Western Region by his administration as well.

Meanwhile, he tried to build the Action Group into an effective nationwide party by making alliances with ethnic groups in other regions. Awolowo supported his party's efforts to accelerate Nigeria's progress toward self-government by pushing the British to commit to an early date for independence. After a disappointing showing in the hard-fought 1959 elections and after the two other major parties had formed a coalition, he became leader of the opposition in the federal House of Representatives. After Nigeria achieved independence in 1960, Awolowo began to modify his earlier position, leaning toward socialism and advocating a neutral foreign policy rather than his earlier pro-Western position.

With dissension growing in his own party over both ideology and administration, Awolowo fought to maintain ascendancy. Although he managed to prevail at the annual party conference in 1962, one year later he was tried and convicted of conspiracy to overthrow the government and was sentenced to 10 years in prison. He was released after a military coup took place in July 1966—the second coup to occur that year.

Later that year Awolowo was a member of the National Conciliation Committee, which attempted to mediate a rift between the federal government and the Eastern Region, which was inhabited predominantly by the Igbo people. Mediation attempts failed, and he eventually threw his support behind the federal government when the region seceded as the Republic of Biafra, sparking civil war (1967–70). During the conflict, Awolowo was federal commissioner for finance and vice chairman of the Federal Executive Council. In the mid-1970s he was chancellor of the University of Ife (now Obafemi Awolowo University) and Ahmadu Bello University.

When the 12-year ban on political activity was lifted in 1978 in preparation for a return to civilian rule, Awolowo emerged as the leader of the Unity Party of Nigeria. He ran for president in the elections of 1979 and 1983 but was defeated both times by Shehu Shagari. Following a military coup at the end of 1983, parties were once again banned, and Awolowo retired from politics.

An important figure in Nigerian history, Awolowo's ideals and accomplishments continue to influence Nigerian politics. He wrote several books, including *Awo: The Autobiography of Chief Obafemi Awolowo* (1960) and *Thoughts on Nigerian Constitution* (1966).

Ahmadu Bello – *Saduana of Sokoto*

Al-Haji Sir Ahmadu Bello (June 12, 1910 - January 15, 1966) was a Nigerian politician, and was the first premier of the Northern Nigeria region from 1954-1966. He is considered to be a founding father of the modern Nigerian nation state, which was formed October 1, 1960 when Bello's NPC forged an alliance with Dr. Nnamdi Azikiwe's NCNC (National Council of Nigeria and the Cameroons) to form Nigeria's first indigenous federal government which led to independence from Britain. Despite his popularity and political support, Bello chose to remain in the North instead of accepting the post of national Prime Minister, which would have required living in the South.

Bello combined traditional leadership qualities with knowledge of Western governance. Bello's greatest legacy was the modernization and unification of the diverse people of Northern Nigeria.

Early life

Ahmadu Bello was born on June 12, 1910, in Rabbah, Sokoto State, the son of a district head and heir to the Sokoto Emirate. His great-grandfather was Sultan Bello, son of the revered Usman Dan Fodio who founded the Fulani Empire, which was the largest in Sub-Saharan Africa. Ahmadu Bello received his education first at the feet of Muslim masters, studying the Quran, the hadith, and Shariah, then at Sokoto Middle School, the only modern school at the time in the Sokoto province (1917-1926).

He then proceeded to the Katsina Teacher's Training College. After spending five years at Katsina, he was appointed by the Sultan as a teacher in his own former school in Sokoto. In 1934, he was made the district head of Rabbah within the Sultan's administration. Four years later, he was promoted and sent to Gusau to become a divisional head. In 1938, he made an unsuccessful bid to become the new Sultan of Sokoto. The successful sultan immediately conferred on him the traditional, now honorary, title of "Sarduna" and elevated him to the Sokoto Native Authority Council. He first became politically active in 1945, when he helped to form a Youth Social Circle, which later (1948) affiliated with the NPC (Northern Peoples Congress) of which he became President-General in 1954. In 1948, he was offered a scholarship to study local government administration in England. Ahmadu Bello took the scholarship, sensing he needed to develop his knowledge about the process of governance.

Nigerian politics

After returning from England, he was nominated to represent the province of Sokoto in the regional House of Assembly, and elected. As a member of the assembly, he was a notable voice for northern interest and embraced a style of consultation and consensus with the major representatives of the northern emirates: Kano, Bornu, and Sokoto. As the movement for independence from the British Empire gathered momentum, Bello emerged as a strong advocate of federalism as the system of government that in his view was most suitable for Nigeria. This was especially attractive to Northern Nigerians, who had a history of sharing power. Nigeria has some 300 clan groups. He may also have wanted to protect the North from what he perceived as the possibility of Southern domination. He also served on the national constitutional drafting commission as a representative of the North.

In the first elections held in Northern Nigeria in 1952, Ahmadu Bello won a seat in the Northern House of Assembly, and became a member of the regional executive council as minister of works. Bello was successively minister of Works, of Local Government, and of Community Development in the Northern Region of Nigeria. In 1953 and in 1957, he led the Northern delegation during independence talks in London.

Premier of the North

In 1954, Bello became the first Premier of Northern Nigeria. In the 1959 independence elections, he led the NPC to win a plurality of the parliamentary seats. Bello's NPC forged an alliance with Dr. Nnamdi Azikiwe's NCNC (National Council of Nigeria and the Cameroons) to form Nigeria's first indigenous federal government which led to independence from Britain. In forming the 1960 independence federal government of the Nigeria, Bello as president of the NPC, chose—although arguably one of the most influential politicians in Nigeria—to remain Premier of Northern Nigeria and devolved the position of Prime Minister of the Federation to the deputy president of the NPC, Abubakar Tafawa Balewa. He apparently did not want to live in Lagos and preferred the political climate of the North from that of the South. His disinclination to head the national government also suggests that he was not interested in power for the sake of power but in serving the people whose votes had elected him to office.

Political achievements

Bello's many political accomplishments include establishing the Northern Regional Development Corporation (NRDC)(subsequently the later the Northern Nigeria Development Corporation (NNDC), the Bank of the North, the Broadcasting Company of Northern Nigeria (BCNN) and the Nigeria Citizen Newspapers. The North was less developed economically than the South, and Bello argued that it was necessary for the North to catch up with the South for the sake of national unity. He traveled constantly across the North, meeting people and listening to their concerns.

Bellow was assassinated during a January 15, 1966, military coup which toppled Nigeria's post-independence government. He was still serving as premier of Northern Nigeria at the time.

Religious practice

Ahmadu Bello was a practicing Muslim. He married five times. In 1955, he performed the Hajj, becoming Alhaji Ahmadu Bello. From then until his death, he visited Mecca annually to perform the Umrah. He walked every day to his local Mosque for prayer. He chose "work and worship" as the slogan for Northern Nigeria. Bello established a reputation for religious toleration. On Christmas Day 1959 he stated, in a broadcast:

Speaking about the vision of Ahmad Bello University, he stated: *The cardinal principle upon which our University is founded is to impart knowledge and learning to men and women of all races without any distinction on the grounds of race, religious, or political beliefs.*

Family

Ahmadu Bello's first wife was Goggon Kurya Hafsatu bint Abdulkadir Maccido, daughter of the Waziri of Sokoto (they married in 1932). His second wife (married 1934, divorced 1938) was Kande. His third was Amiru Fadima (married 1934, divorced 1938). His fourth wife (married 1940) was Goggon Kano Amina bint Abubakar, daughter of the District Head of Bici. His fifth wife was Jabbo bint Aliyu, daughter of the Sarkin Yaki of Gwandu (married 1949). In 1952, he married Jabbo bint Aliyu, daughter of the Sarkin Yaki of Gwandu.

Legacy

Bello's greatest legacy was the modernization and unification of the diverse people of Northern Nigeria. He was awarded several honorary doctorates, including the Doctor of Law from UNN (University of Nigeria Nsukka) in December 1961. He was honored by the country from which he had helped to negotiate independence, being made a Knight of the British Empire (KBE) by Queen Elizabeth II in 1959 just before the end of colonial rule.

He founded the Ahmadu Bello University (1962) in Zaria, the second largest University in Africa, which is named after him. He was the University's first Chancellor. Nigeria's 200 naira carries his portrait. There is a 1995 biography about his first wife, Hafsatu Ahmadu Bello, who was slain alongside him. His **assassination,** for which members of the **Igbo** tribe were responsible, was one of the factors that led to the subsequent Civil War (1967-1970) when the Southern province of Biafra attempted to secede. He wanted both national and Pan-African unity. He did not waste time blaming the ills of his time on **colonialism,** but instead set out to develop his region and to adapt from the West what suited Nigeria, while retaining those cultural practices and values that were cherished and integral to Nigerian identity.

Yakubu Gowon

Alternative Title: Jack Gowon

Yakubu Gowon, also known as **Jack Gowon** (born October 19, 1934, Pankshin, Nigeria), Nigerian military leader, who served as head of state (1966–75).

From Plateau state in the middle belt of Nigeria, Gowon's father was an early convert to Christianity. Gowon was educated in Zaria and later became a career army officer. He was trained in Ghana and in England at Sandhurst and twice served in the Congo region as part of Nigeria's peacekeeping force there in the early 1960s. After the coup of January 1966, he was appointed chief of staff by Major General Johnson Aguiyi-Ironsi, the new leader. Northern officers staged a countercoup in July 1966, and Gowon emerged as the compromise head of the new government.

Gowon tried to resolve the ethnic tensions that threatened to fatally divide Nigeria. Although he was eventually successful in ending attacks against Igbo in the north, he was unable to affect a more lasting peace. In a final attempt to resolve the conflict, on May 27, 1967, Gowon declared a state of emergency and divided Nigeria's four regions into 12 states. Three days later the Eastern region declared itself the independent state of Biafra with Odumegwu Ojukwu as its leader; armed conflict began in July.

Gowon directed government forces to remember that they were essentially fighting Nigerians, who were to be encouraged to rejoin the country. He also allowed a team of international observers to monitor the conduct of his troops. After the government victory in January 1970, a remarkable reconciliation took place between victors and vanquished, largely attributable to Gowon's personal influence. By the mid-1970s Gowon was emerging as an international leader and was involved in the establishment of the Economic Community of West African States (ECOWAS). On July 29, 1975, however, while Gowon was in Uganda for an Organization- of_African Unity summit meeting, the army removed him from office.

Gowon was exiled to Great Britain. He was stripped of his rank for allegedly participating in the assassination of his successor, Murtala Mohammed, in 1976. He was pardoned by Shehu_Shagari in 1981, and his rank was restored by Ibrahim Babangida in

1987. Having earned a Ph.D. at Warwick University in 1983, he became a professor of political science at the University of Jos in the mid-1980s and attained the status of an elder statesman of Nigerian politics.

Ikemba Chukwuemeka odimegwu Ojukwu

Odumegwu Ojukwu, in full **Chief Chukwuemeka Odumegwu Ojukwu** (born November 4, 1933, Zungeru, Nigeria—died November 26, 2011, London, England), Nigerian military leader and politician, who was head of the secessionist state of Biafra during the Nigerian civil war.
Ojukwu was the son of a successful Igbo businessman. After graduating from the University of Oxford in 1955, he returned to Nigeria to serve as an administrative officer. After two years, however, he joined the army and was rapidly promoted thereafter.

In January 1966 a group of largely Igbo junior army officers overthrew Nigeria's civilian government but then were forced to hand power to the highest-ranking military officer, Major General T.U. Johnson Aguiyi-Ironsi (also an Igbo); he appointed Lieutenant Colonel Ojukwu as military governor of the mostly Igbo Eastern region. However, Hausa and Yoruba army officers from the Northern and Western regions feared a government dominated by the Igbo, and in July 1966 northern officers staged a successful countercoup in which Lieutenant Colonel (later General) Yakubu Gowon was installed as the new head of state. Under Gowon's rule, Ojukwu retained his command of the Eastern region.

Meanwhile, the rising tide of feeling against the Igbo in the Northern region led to large-scale massacres of Igbos by northerners in May–September 1966.
The Eastern region felt increasingly alienated from the federal military government under Gowon. Ojukwu's main proposal to end the ethnic strife was a significant devolution of power to the regions. The federal government initially agreed to this solution at a conference in January 1967 but then rejected it soon afterward. Ojukwu responded in March–April 1967 by separating the Eastern regional government's administration and revenues from those of the federal government.

Mounting secessionist pressures from his fellow Igbo finally compelled Ojukwu on May 30, 1967, to declare the Eastern region an independent sovereign state as the Republic of Biafra. Federal troops soon afterward invaded Biafra, and civil war broke out in July 1967. Ojukwu led Biafra's unsuccessful struggle to survive as an independent state throughout the civil war, and on the eve of Biafra's surrender in 1970, he fled to Côte d'Ivoire, where he was granted asylum.

Ojukwu remained in exile until 1982, when he was pardoned and returned to Nigeria. He joined the National Party of Nigeria (NPN) in January 1983 and subsequently attempted to reenter politics; his bid for the senate representing the state of Anambra was unsuccessful. He was detained for 10 months following a coup that brought Muhammad Buhari to power at the end of 1983. In 1993 he once again joined a political party, this time the Social Democratic Party, but he was disqualified from running for president.

A member of constitutional conferences in 1993 and again from 1994 to 1995, he, along with other former Nigerian leaders, was consulted in 1998 by Abdusalam Abubakar, the military head of state, as Nigeria once again began the process of converting from military to civilian rule. In 2003 Ojukwu, representing a new political party that he helped form, the All Progressive Grand Alliance, unsuccessfully ran for president. He ran again in 2007 but was defeated by the ruling party's candidate, Umaru Yar'Adua, in an election that was strongly criticized by international observers as being marred by voting irregularities.

The early years of Nigerian independence were difficult for the country. Political turmoil, riots, and ethnic rivalries resulted in a civil war in the latter half of the 1960s. Members of the largest ethnic group, the Ibos, were murdered in great numbers during the chaos, and more than a million (some sources say over four million) survivors fled back to their homeland in eastern Nigeria. Odumegwu Ojukwu, the military governor of the region, assumed control in the mid-1960s in an attempt to strengthen the bargaining power of the Ibos. He first argued against secession from Nigeria by the Ibos and, instead, urged easterners to accept a loosening of ties with the rest of Nigeria. A 1968 article in *Time* magazine stated, "[Odumegwu Ojukwu] was a calm and reasoned voice pleading for a united Nigeria long after other powerful Ibos had angrily given up hope of preserving the union." Critics felt that because most of Odumegwu Ojukwu's inheritance from his father was in Lagos, he had a personal stake in keeping Nigeria together.

Odumegwu Ojukwu changed his stance, however, and sided with the separatists on the issue of safety for the Ibos. At one point, he and Nigerian army chief of staff Yakubu Gowon, also in control of the central Nigerian government, appeared to be nearing a compromise that would have allowed the Ibos a measure of autonomy while staying within the Nigerian federation. But Gowon was unwilling to let the eastern region maintain a separate army, and Odumegwu Ojukwu was unsure of the ability of the Nigerian central government to protect the Ibos. Odumegwu Ojukwu reluctantly demanded independence for the easterners. He formally proclaimed the independent Republic of Biafra on May 30, 1967, during a reception in the regional capital of Enugu. At the time, he also hinted that the Nigerian central government had played a role in the genocide of the Ibo people. He then built up his army and expelled northerners from Biafra, telling them that, because of the flood of Ibo refugees, non-easterners should leave for their own safety.

Civil War

At the onset of conflict in 1967, Odumegwu Ojukwu received little sympathy or support from the international community. Nigeria, however, was backed by Britain, the Soviet Union, and most of Western Europe. The Nigerian central government first established a naval blockade along the Biafran coast then sent troops, composed mostly of Muslims from the northern part of the country, to the east where they were met by Odumegwu Ojukwu's rebel forces. Initially, the Biafrans took control of strategic points in the midwestern region of Nigeria and the oil-rich Niger River delta. The central government retaliated by sending in more armed forces, which escalated the conflict into a full-blown civil war. Odumegwu Ojukwu directed the overall strategy for Biafra in the war, but he left most of the tactical decisions to his brigade commanders and often sought advice from Ibo elders. He downplayed his role in the civil war, although the Nigerians frequently called the conflict "Ojukwu's war" and depicted the military leader as a power-mad Hitler who was shattering the unity of the new Nigeria. Odumegwu Ojukwu told *New York Times Magazine* reporter Lloyd Garrison, "Independence is not one man getting up and declaring it. Freedom without substance is meaningless."

By the end of 1967, Nigerian forces had regained control of the midwest and had cut off Biafran access to the sea. Although they had encircled the Biafrans, they were unable to penetrate the Ibo heartland. The Biafrans, however, were crowded into mangrove swamps and hardwood forests, unable to provide themselves with the materials of daily existence. Meanwhile, Soviet-built warplanes, many flown by hired Egyptians and British pilots, cut supply lines and inflicted heavy casualties during raids on Biafran urban centers.

Consequently, Biafrans were starving to death at a rate conservatively estimated to be approximately 1, 000 people a day, according to *Time*. Other sources estimate that as many as 8, 000 people a day died of starvation in the region during this time. Despite the hardship, the Ibo people continued to support the war effort. Odumegwu Ojukwu thus began waging a public-relations campaign to receive badly needed supplies from the rest of the world. He sent out press releases and photos showing starving Biafrans. He persuaded several countries, including Czechoslovakia, The Netherlands, and Belgium, to cut off weapons supplies to Nigeria. Odumegwu Ojukwu hoped for airlifts, which he considered a symbol of the world helping a besieged people. But by October of 1969, realizing that he would receive little foreign support, he appealed for United Nations mediation to obtain terms for a cease fire and to begin peace negotiations. The Nigerian central government, however, was not inclined to accept anything less than surrender and seemed to consider starvation a weapon of war that would preclude its having to send soldiers into battle. At about this time, Odumegwu Ojukwu told *Time* correspondent James Wilde, "What you are seeing now is the end of a long, long journey. It began in the far north of Nigeria and moved steadily southward as we were driven out of place after place. Now this path has become the road to the slaughterhouse here in the Ibo heartland." By the end of the year, 120, 000 Nigerian troops had divided Biafra in half. The rebel nation collapsed in January of 1970.

After the civil war, under Gowon's supervision, the Nigerian central government took steps to ensure that the Ibos would be treated as fellow citizens rather than defeated enemies. Programs were developed to reintegrate the Ibos into a united Nigeria. Many Biafran military officers rejoined the central government as part of a general amnesty. Odumegwu Ojukwu, however, opted for voluntary exile and went to the Ivory Coast on the invitation of that nearby African nation's president. He justified his actions at the time by declaring, as quoted in *Newsweek,* "Whilst I live, Biafra lives." Odumegwu Ojukwu was invited back to Nigeria by Shehu Shagari of the Nigerian government in 1982. Since then, the former Biafran leader has become active in the National Party of Nigeria. Although he was unsuccessful in a bid to be elected to the national senate, his advice is often sought by factions of the Nigerian and greater African community. He has encouraged the military to support Nigeria's slow transition toward democracy. In 1993, he publicly supported Nigeria's Republican Party because he thought it would be the best guarantor of eastern interests in national politics.

Ojukwu had several honours and titles bestowed upon him during his life, including the honorary chieftaincy title Ikemba of Nnewi.

Herbert Samuel Macualey

Olayinka Herbert Samuel Heelas Badmus Macaulay (14 November 1864 – 7 May 1946) was a Nigerian nationalist, politician, engineer, architect, journalist, and musician and is considered by many Nigerians as the founder of Nigerian nationalism

Herbert Macaulay was born in Broad St., Lagos on 14 November 1864 to the family of Thomas Babington Macaulay and Abigail Crowther. His parents were children of people captured from what is now Nigeria, resettled in Sierra Leone by the British West Africa Squadron, and eventual returnees to present day Nigeria. Thomas Babington Macaulay was one of the sons of Ojo Oriare while Abigail Crowther was the daughter of Bishop Samuel Ajayi Crowther, a descendant of King Abiodun. Thomas Babington Macaulay was the founder of the first secondary school in Nigeria, the CMS Grammar School, Lagos.

Macaulay entered primary school in 1869 and from 1869 to 1877, he was educated at St Paul's Breadfruit School, Lagos and CMS Faji School, Lagos. From 1877 to October 1880, he attended CMS Grammar School, Lagos for his secondary education. He was a student at the school when his father died in 1878. In 1880, he joined his maternal uncles trade steamer and embarked on a trade and missionary journey across the Niger River visiting Bonny, Lokoja, Gbebe and Brass. After going to a Christian missionary school, he took a job as a clerical assistant and indexer at the Department of Public Works, Lagos. Thereafter, with the support of the colonial administration, Macaulay left Lagos on July 1, 1890 to further his training in England. From 1891 to 1894 he studied civil engineering in Plymouth, England and was also a pupil under of G.D. Bellamy, a borough surveyor and water engineer in Plymouth. In 1893, he became a graduate of the Royal Institute of British Architects, London. Macaulay was also an accomplished musician who received a certificate in music from Trinity College, London and a certificate in violin playing from Music International College, London.

Career

Upon his return to Lagos in September 1893, he resumed work with the colonial service as a surveyor of Crown Lands. He left the service as land inspector in September 1898 due to growing distaste for the British rule over the Lagos Colony and the position of Yorubaland and the Niger Coast Protectorate as British colonies in all but name. Other authors such as Patrick Dele-Cole have noted the abuse of office allegations (leveled by his British superiors) and pursuit of private gain controversy that clouded Macaulay's resignation as surveyor of Crown Grants. Kristin Mann, citing British

Colonial Government dispatches notes that Macaulay behaved dishonestly, by using "his position as Surveyor of Crown Lands to help friends acquire crown grants and persecute enemies by granting their land to others". She further writes that Macaulay "obtained crown grants under false names and then sold them at a profit". In October 1898, he obtained a license to practice as a surveyor. As a surveyor, his plans and valuations included E.J. Alex Taylor's house on Victoria St, Henry Carr's residence in Tinubu, Akinola Maja's house and Doherty villa in Campos Square.

Private life

Macaulay married Caroline Pratt, daughter of an African Superintendent of Police in December 1898. Their marriage came to an end in August 1899 upon Caroline's death during childbirth and Macaulay is reported to have vowed never to marry again. While Macaulay never remarried in the Church, he had mistresses from whom he had a number of children, as well as companionships which bore no children (Sarah Coker, daughter of JPL Davies and Sarah Forbes Bonetta lived with Macaulay from 1909 until her death in 1916). Macaulay was reportedly the first Nigerian to own a motor car.

Though from a family of devout Anglicans, Macaulay embraced indigenous African religious traditions, was superstitious, and dabbled in the practice of magic. His personal papers contain notes from fortune tellers and diviners with instructions around taboos, divinations, sacrifices, and other occult practices. Macaulay was also a member of the Association of Babalawos (Ifa priests) of Lagos.

Macaulay was a great socialite in Victorian Lagos. He organized concerts at his residence (named "Kirsten Hall" after his German Consul friend Arthur Kirsten) on 8 Balbina Street in Yaba. Macaulay was nicknamed "Wizard of Kirsten Hall" because of his ability to obtain classified information. Macaulay ran a network of informants who he paid handsomely. Many times, minutes from colonial government minutes would be leaked in newspapers that Macaulay was associated with. Whole sections of colonial government files and telegrams can be found in the *Maculay Papers* at the Africana section of the Library at the University of Ibadan.

As an opponent of British rule

Prior to the beginning of the twentieth century, Macaulay associated with many Lagos socialites, worked as a private surveyor and had a moderate outlook about colonialism. However, by the end of the 1900s, he had begun to veer from his professional and social activities to become a political activist. He joined the Anti-Slavery and Aborigines' Protection Society. Macaulay was an unlikely champion of the masses. A grandson of Ajayi Crowther, the first African bishop of the Niger Territory, he was born into a Lagos that was divided politically into groups arranged in a convenient pecking order – the British rulers who lived in the posh Marina district, the Saros and other slave descendants who lived to the west, and the Brazilians who lived behind the whites in the Portuguese Town. Behind all three lived the real Lagosians, the masses of indigenous Yoruba people, disliked and generally ignored by their privileged neighbours. It was not until Macaulay's generation that the Saros and Brazilians even began to contemplate making common cause with the masses.

Macaulay was one of the first Nigerian nationalists and for most of his life a strong opponent of many colonial policies. As a reaction to claims by the British that they were governing with "the true interests of the natives at heart", he wrote: "The dimensions of "the true interests of the natives at heart" are algebraically equal to the length, breadth and depth of the whiteman's pocket." In 1908 he exposed European corruption in the handling of railway finances and in 1919 he argued successfully for the chiefs whose land had been taken by the British in front of the Privy Council in London. As a result, the colonial government was forced to pay compensation to the chiefs.

In 1909, he came out publicly against the prohibition of spirits into Nigeria which he felt will ultimately lead to reduced government revenues and thereafter increased taxation. Macaulay also found himself in opposition to the colonial government in three major issues that were prominent in Lagos life during 1900-1930. The issues included the proposed water rate, selection of the Oba of Lagos and the Imamate of the Lagos Central Mosque. Macaulay opposed colonial taxation to fund water supply in Lagos on the grounds of taxation without representation. He was a major supporter of the House of Docemo in Lagos. Largely because Lagos was not under indirect rule, the Oba of Lagos unlike many of its counterparts in other areas of the country was stripped of many of his traditional authorities. Macaulay supported the House of Docemo in its opposition to the water rate and colonial acquisition of Lagos lands. He also galvanized the Ilu Committee composed of the Oba of Lagos and traditional chiefs in Lagos to oppose some of the colonial policies.

Macaulay's profile in Lagos was enhanced by the Oluwa Land case. Amodu Tijani Oluwa, a traditional chief, had challenged the compulsory acquisition without compensation of his family land in Apapa. He lost his appeal at the Supreme Court and took the case to the Privy Court Council in London. Macaulay was Oluwa's private secretary in the trip to London. Oluwa's case was supported by the Ilu Committee and the Oba who were interested in the protection of their family lands in Lagos. In London, Macaulay presented himself as Oluwa's private secretary and as a representative of the Oba and in the capacity he made statements which the colonial authorities felt were inimical to their interest. In 1920, the Eleko, Eshungbayi was ostracized by the British because he refused to disavow allegations against the colonial authorities made by Macaulay in London.

To further his political activities, Macaulay co-founded the Nigerian Daily News, a platform he used to write opinion pieces such as Justitia Fiat: The Moral Obligation of the British Government to the House of Docemo. He also wrote a piece titled Henry Carr Must Go. From 1923 to 1938, he became a prominent figure in many important political issues in Lagos including the elections into the quinquennial elections into the Legislative Council, triennial elections to the Lagos Town Council, and the headship of the House of Docemo. In his political activities, he relied on the Lagos Daily News, the Lagos Market Women Association led by his ally, Alimotu Pelewura, the House of Docemo and many uneducated Lagosians. His political opinions divided many Lagos elites as he used the Daily News to publicly vilify his opponents and former friends such as Henry Carr, Macaulay became very popular and on 24 June 1923 he founded the Nigerian National Democratic Party (NNDP), the first Nigerian political party. The party won all the seats in the elections of 1923, 1928 and 1933. Though, the party's major function was to put candidates into the legislative council, it had a broader objective of promoting democracy in Nigeria, increasing higher Nigerian participation in the social, economic and educational development of Nigeria. Though, the party wanted to be national in outlook, Macaulay's strength of support was from the House of Docemo and therefore his preoccupation with the defense of the House of Docemo and his desire to control the party limited the growth of the party.

As a supporter of the British

In 1931 relations between Macaulay and the British began to improve up to the point that the governor even held conferences with Macaulay. In October 1938 the more radical Nigerian Youth Movement fought and won elections for the Lagos Town Council, ending the dominance of Macaulay and his National Democratic Party.

Legal problems

Macaulay was barred from running for public office because of legal problems - he was convicted twice by the British Colonial Government in Lagos; the first time for fraud, and the second time for sedition.

Misappropriation of funds

After going into private practice as a surveyor and architect, Macaulay faced some financial difficulty and misappropriated funds from an estate he served as executor for. His actions were uncovered by the authorities who tried him and sentenced him to two years in prison. The historian Patrick Dele-Cole outlines evidence suggesting that Macaulay was unfairly persecuted at his 1913 trial. The prosecuting counsel, one Robert Irving, was Herbert Macaulay's tenant who may have pursued a private vendetta. Macaulay had obtained a court order to evict Robert Irving on December 3, 1912. Additionally, Macaulay's lawyers encountered severe difficulties putting up a solid defense in the course of the case: as an example Macaulay's lawyers were unable to find the police magistrate anywhere in Lagos to obtain bail. Other incidents include the acting Chief Justice fining Macaulay £100 despite the five assessors in the court returning a not guilty verdict. Cole also underscores Macaulay's scrupulous transparency regarding the trust. According to Cole "the will of the testatrix was read in public at the request of Macaulay and the loan he obtained in order the clear the debts of the testatrix was explained to the beneficiaries of the will (Macaulay's niece was the principal beneficiary and she certainly did not engage Irving to prosecute the case), yet he was convicted of 'intent to defraud'". Finally, Cole notes that Macaulay's sentence of five years was "unusually severe".

PART 3

WHAT ARE YOUR PERSONAL AND NATIONAL GOALS?

-To Succeed With Happiness in Life You Must Have a Long Term Goal!-

A nation, like a person, to be truly successful and prosperous, must be able to at least set-out short-term and long-term goals; upon these set-out goals, the nation's or person's entire life should oscillate or revolve. The short-term goals serve as a compass, which will guide and guard you across the vast oceans, space and time to achieve and embrace the set-out long-term goals! Without that, the nation or person becomes a puppet for the Spirits; a pendulum dangling from left to right, front to back and vice versa. That is the major problem with most nations as with most people of this awesome world; lack of or insufficient focus and definite goals. Nigeria and her citizens are evidently in the same rut! Biafra should better set out a short-term and long-term leadership goals and objectives in order to avoid unwanted future issues taking hold of the system governing the people.

No more wars; No more fighting; now is the time for Biafra peace and harmony. Yes we can!

Time has come for Biafrans to begin to cut-off all the shorts-cuts they have being encouraging among them for long and face reality head-on.

Biafrans in this era has grown beyond wisdom; most have grown so much to embody wisdom themselves through divine help or the dint of their hard work. Therefore, human beings of this era had grown somehow wise enough to know what is right or wrong.

Time has come for us to stop cheating, lying, keeping secrets and hoarding the free flow of natural information. Doing things in these ways shortens, suffocates and pollutes the essence of love, peace and harmony. Reason my people; wisdom will set you free from your mental bondage.

In the end, what shall it add to your life to own more than you need? All you can receive for all that hassle to accumulate material things is more of an added stress, strain and distress! Stop imposing rules and regulations upon yourselves; because you are not the 'Creator' but the created. For the sake of love, peace and harmony, I suggest that humanity should go back to their roots and embrace on the rules of the instinct; the rule from the living conscience; that is the natural rules that humans are made with and should duly obey for positive and balanced progress to prevail among nations and global community as one.

When people or any living thing are left free to think and reason through instincts, their thinking and reasoning ability quickly connects in harmony with the inner source or habit-force which embodies all human senses be it good or bad, in this mindset, life and living is awesome.

For your spiritual empowerments to foster, let out Man-Made rules and let in Natural-Made Rules!

IDEAL LIFE AND A BALANCED SYSTEM OF LEADERSHIP FOR BIAFRA

The decision you make and the action you take, is synonymous with the life you live, and of that which you will keep living and giving. So decide and act positive; no other way out to excellence.

After all said and done; the daunting question should be: '**what is the essence of governance for you as a leader? Is it to lead your people towards the protocol of love, peace and harmony; as, to enable them savor the hidden benefits which are replete in the path to love, peace, and unity in harmony?** Or *does true governance mean to lead your obedient people: to war, to kill and be killed; to hate and vandalize, cheat and deceive; leaving them with the sure repercussions such trait of character carry and distribute along with them?*

Whatever your personal answer may be to the above questions, I advise you to think it out well over before you decide and act.

However, for me, my candid view is that, every living being or thing has got just, two basic choices in their everyday life; and these two choices fundamentally, determine their own essence of life; their character trait, their general concepts and choices of values. In our everyday lives, we are confronted with some looming obligations to do either this or that; to deny this or to accept that; to delete or to save; and to go or to stay…

If that is the immutable reality of our everyday lives, we are obliged to live with such constant moments of decision-making and choice taking through to the very last of our respective days, here on Earth! Take your decisions with prudence and act with caution.

In addition, this tricky question popped up from nowhere on my mental screen asking: **'after all said and done, in time to reckon and to give an account for the deeds and activities which we carried out when we have the liberty to decode and choose; what then for you, is the essence of life?**

Is it to spend most of your life in schools; at work and in desperate pursuit of material wealth and fame; with their inevitable negative repercussions? On the other hand, does life also mean for you: love, peace and harmony with yourself, family, neighbors, and other people; together with the things of creation in general; and the guaranteed benefits they carry along with them?

You presume and accepted that, 'your destiny is in your hands', why then must you obediently continue to do things which you are often asked to do; more than those things which you really would want to do, which are yearning and yelling for attention from your deeper mind? Before you answer, take a walk on one side; look inside out of you while you think it well over.

In summary, to be able to govern or lead people smoothly, you must be able to learn to govern or lead yourself firstly; your family and friends to find love, peace and harmony. In the absence of learning to govern and lead yourself harmoniously, you can never be able to govern or lead others well enough to achieve love, peace and harmony of which you were unable to achieve on your own. **These are the ultimate goals of all people; to find, during their lifetime: love, good health, peace and harmony!**

Concisely, it is obvious that, human beings, in the long history of their continued existence on this Earth, have always had the freedom to decide and choose. Nevertheless, sadly, I lack the knowledge of any era in these long histories of human race marked by this kind of: peace, love and harmony, which I am making, reference to, in this book. **I refer to the kind of: love, peace and harmony which you can achieve only through the dint of hard inner-work; the looming task of deciding and choosing which begins and ends our everyday lives.** I, also, refer to the kind of: love, peace and harmony you alone can find, use and feel, for yourself alone; through all your given organs: your sight, tongue, ears, nose and your central nervous system.

Sincerely speaking, my long years of experience and understanding of the simple, but complicated protocol of: love, peace and harmony with that of the Creation, I can stake anything that, our global government or system of leadership was designed and structured on the wrong premise. Our national and global leadership is pathetically trailing on the wrong pathway to life and, now, find them entangled in the mesh of complications, illusion and dissatisfaction.

The national insecurity, the crisis, the discrimination and terrorism are some of the obvious manifestations of how far away we are distancing ourselves; our born and unborn children from the path leading to the only valuable things of this life: love, peace and harmony, which, we are wrongly searching everyday in diverse and frenetic, if not ridiculous ways.

No doubt we need money because we designed money; awesome! **Nevertheless, the hard knock question is, for what do we really need this money, is it for fame and all the material wealth we accumulate?** Is it to find and accumulate: love, peace, good health and harmony or to find and buy Houses, food, clothes and fame? *Obviously, you have sought and found houses, food, clothes and caprice; but have you equally found: love, peace, sound health and harmony in all these long years of human history?* Think this well over before you give your opinions.

IGBO ANCESTORS AND VIEWS ON MODERN CIVILIZATION

Because of the mental and economic wealth of the Igbos, everybody is borne rich with enough positive cultural inheritance. In those days as I remember, even without the "precarious oil boom that devastated the Biafraland and which benefited the Nigerian nation that was amalgamated as one nation by the colonial imperialists". Before then, our grandparents had already established a powerful and rich system of life for themselves and for their posterity, which was founded on a natural and solid ground. They had everything nature could offer for all forms of self sustainable-life; they believed in one God but, still had the liberty to choose how best to worship God; they were practical enough to formulate a durable and peace sustaining system of government which was able to bind the entire Igbo race together in genealogical orders of: family, kindred, community, tribes and region, and comprising of everyone within their occupied lands without favor; discrimination or disrespect;, all things being equal. They also worshipped one God –Chukwu; Chineke or ¨Chukwu Abiama¨ ardent believers in the living God who, they worshipped and communed through symbols and figures with a deep feeling of divine present always around them.

The Igbo ancestors were also clever enough to allow their lives to revolve under the evergreen and everlasting shelter of Mother-Nature; their medicine, their food, their drinks, their houses were provided for and readily available without leaving the vicinity of their natural habitat. They had an enviable understanding of their prospects in the world; they lived against all odds without disrupting the course of things of creation; their lifestyle was in utmost harmony with the entire ecosystem; eating and dinning with the devil, with the angels, jungle and domestic animals. They always had enough food and charity to give and share; they were obviously analphabets but their technological, scientific and humanistic achievements supersede in many ways today's modern realizations on one-to-on, in a deeper sense.

What I so much admired about our ancestors was the fact that everyone among them was completely independent! They freely shared their knowledge over all created things without conditions or reservations; made their houses by themselves, beds, farms, track-roads, utensils and weapons for self defense. Virtually everything: clothing, booze, and medicine etc. Great generation they were! They were my true heroes; my idols! They made their own laws guiding, guarding and binding them together. Those rules still exist today as customs or traditions which we classify as 'customary laws' and in some places they refer to them as 'community laws'. Their lives had moved on smoothly in this order till the advent of the missionaries and colonialist.

Advent of Colonialism in Biafra/Africa

As a writer, I never like quoting historical data; I rather prefer to write out of my personal observations, analysis of events of the day as I see and feel them on that spur of the moment. Having said that, I want you to forgive me if I fail to enumerate exact historical figures and names of our colonial peoples' and their varied activities in African continent of which the defunct Biafra is one according to facts and figures evidenced along the line of history.

From what I remembered or bothered to remember from history, the colonial masters brought education, Christianity and many other good things to the continent of Africa, which my beloved Biafra happened to be one.

I learnt that, Mongo Park discovered River Niger; and that Christopher Columbus discovered Africa and so many such misleading historical facts. As a child, I was wondering how someone could come all the way from another

continent so far away, to find and discover a place already being inhabited by people. How could that be for real? I used to secretly wonder within my layman's mental enclave if those people living in such places then, have no eyes to see that big ocean meandering ceaselessly across their region where they settled; as in the case of River Niger for example? Or they never known or seen an ocean in any ways? Well the history has been written to favor the writers because my fore-fathers were unable to develop reading or writing skills! The above examples among many others, form part and parcel of the present adverse situation which has befallen our entire world; our colonists deliberately failed to lay the true story or history of things bare for all to see and when they do lay facts, they nearly always find favorable ways to distort given facts to their unique advantage.

Of course, the colonial masters or missionaries as they were best referred to brought with them lots of good things and also, took away lots of good things. The sad mistake they made was to condemn, annihilate and belittle all the good things that they found their respective colonies doing before their arrival or emergence. It would have been wiser or prudent to blend the good things of the people and allow those things that were good to grow and foster and endure, so that, today, the posterity will also be able to read and know those good things of their ancestors- but, today, what do the majority of Africans know about their ancestors? Nearly only the wrongs things, the negative and dark things as if the African people are all wrong, dark and negative; as if their lives were not worth the pain and energy of documentation in the good book of world history. That was a deliberate and dangerous oversight; justice not only delayed but totally denied. And that will continue to inflame the anger of many as myself whenever they discover most of those past lies and negative manipulations after being made to wander in the dark for years through inappropriate academic and religious indoctrination.

For such deliberate omissions from our colonial lords, I believe, for the world to achieve peaceful, balanced and harmonious success and progress in all their campaigns for a united and proactive 'One-World' for this to be achieved, the history of the world will have to be rewritten with sincerity and honesty; the deliberate omissions corrected in order to refill the historical vacuum lingering generation after generation.

Ancestor's Views

When look back my days as a child, I remembered most of the conflicts between my biological father and my grandparents; especially, my grandfather who used to complain about the trend and ways of life of the generation of my biological parents who had the fortune or misfortune to live in the era of colonial masters with their education, concept and religion.

In those days not long past, my grandparents used to think simply that, the generation of my biological parents were not doing things and living their lives in productive ways as to make themselves self-reliant, more useful to their respective communities and to their nation in general.

Forty-five-years ago, my Grand-Pa and his mates already predicted the catastrophic future yet to befall "Nigeria as a nation if we continue to live and act the way we are doing" they observed. And that was based on the negative ways they found their growing children carrying out their respective and collective commitments with and to life; as a result of their colonial indoctrination and brainwash...

According to my ancestors- our civilization and life-objectives were forty percent genuine and sixty percent bullshit! They were therefore, simply appalled by what they visualized Forty-five years ago happening and those imminent in our great nation Nigeria! They did not only think, but, there were very emphatic that our generation is heading towards self-inflicted doom; bunch of incompetent parasites; those among others were their sincere feeling about our present education and outlook to life in general.

My grandparents were of the opinion that – No honest human could dedicate a whole life doing just one or two things at the expense of all the others. They were constantly questioning and opposed to the wisdom and the satisfaction in the long run doing just one thing, who will take care of the rest for you; knowing that "human wants are insatiable", knowing also that, "genuine humans are nomads and not sedentary". As experts in their little portion of the world, they also knew very well that doing one thing for long is monotonous, and that monotony can cause serious mental and physical damages such as: depression, which leads to lack of enthusiasm and lack of auto-esteem. And with monotony at that point, your minds will be inundated with ingenious alibi and cliché defending your respective short-comings in the race for life and death. When tangled in situations as the above majority of humans begin to see life as a mess; they tend to question and abuse the Creator; discard honesty and endorse corruption. And all those can only but create a huge vacuum in people's minds which can only be filled by the devil. Such is what is wrong with today's world– full of honorable nincompoops, sycophants, hypocrites who are betraying and assassinating one another in order to cover their weaknesses which were imbibed through laziness, ignorance and mischief" Shakespeare had a similar concept which lead him to say that "human needs are like a pin in a haystack, you will spend all day searching, and when you finally find it, it will not be worth the search".

With this human characteristics in mind, my grandparents believed that "for every man and woman to be real, they must be able to cultivate versatility, keep moving and revolving with time and changes because nothing remains the same,

therefore, to expend this precious and infinite human energy to: learn little, know little and do little, is tantamount to a serious crime against –Chukwu Abiama- the Creator; they opined.

BIAFRAN YOUTH FROM THE NINETEEN-SEVENTYS'

It is true that you can only give what you have. our parents in the Biafran context gave and are still giving to their children the much they have got to offer but unfortunately, their very much is not good enough; so lacking and deficient that we are forced to panic for the huge gap of uncertainty looming over our immediate and far future.

Having lived through the Seventy's to this present time as an adult, I could understand the worries and wisdom of my grandfather; why he was then busy teaching us, his grand children, the very essence of self sufficiency and self dependence. For instance, my grandfather was always taking us to almost everywhere he went during those days: showing, teaching and explaining everything he was doing to enable us, his grand children, to be able to duplicate and replicate those things in the future as and when we grow up into adulthoods; according to him- "that was the right and only feasible way to show us, children how to live a progressive, balanced and fulfilled life".

My grand-pa and his mates taught us many things ranging from: how to make rafters, roof-sheets made from palm fronds or leaves; how to mix red soils to build mud houses, tap palm wine, build cane beds and chairs, fetch fire-woods, transform palm-wine into first, second and third grade alcohol (spirit), sharpen knives on stones with water, grind seeds on stone against stone for cooking; and how to cut trees with cutlasses, hunt animals for food, plow the soil and plant yams, cassavas! And all that was to prepare us ahead of the future, to give us the correct knowledge of how to fend for ourselves and be conscious of the innumerable challenges looming in our distant future. My grandpa and his mates also thought us: the different uses and functions of all types of leaves and roots to cure our sicknesses, wounds and for physical body maintenance; how to transform Palm-Oil into Soaps for bathing and for washing; correct eating habits and the importance of hard work and adequate rest!

Virtually, they gave us very useful education which was aimed at boosting our respective self esteem, enthusiasm and love and satisfaction for life.

The generation of my grandparents was so awesome I can't stop wishing to revive those glorious days and great humans. The people from my Grand Father's generation were my real idols; I must confess because their style of life and education method was most practical!

Modern-day Parenting in Biafraland

What did our biological parents teach us in exchange? Nothing of their own because they have nothing to offer except sending us to missionary school in where I was thought many strange far reaching things: Biology without animals nor plants, laboratory nor tools except imported books with theories and definitions which I struggled hard to comprehend, physics and chemistry without laboratory nor chemicals to give a clue of what was been thought etc. Geography of the world without an idea of my immediate village much less my beloved country Nigeria; and worse still, without a map of the world within sight in a geography class lessons and so forth.

We were thought the history of the world when I knew absolutely nothing about my immediate village, or of our beloved country- except for the little I saw in the street, deciphered out of childish imagination, and those which I learnt from my grand-pa and his mates. Thanks to them!

Worst of all, we were taught Religion based on the principles of the Holy-Bible as the only religion worth the pain. No rooms for CHINEKE, OLUWA, OSALOBUA, etc. (those were the names of the Omni-Potent Creator worshiped by my ancestors as the only God known or imagined to/by them in the same way as can reckon with the Holy-Bible).

Today, so soon, the generation of my grandfather has gradually faded away; no more references whatsoever of their magnanimous presence, impact or existence in the contemporary Nigeria as in the rest of African nations. We have been surreptitiously divested of our ancestral wisdom!

During all those periods from the seventies' upwards, my confusion and frustration had remained deep and immense. The national and global governing bodies somehow created long distance between me and my grand-parents as time progressed. By the time I could realize what was happening to me, my biological father threw my young 'ass' into a boarding house for a better education complying to the then national beliefs in the Nigerian growing system of government. Of course, it was and still is nice to know how to read and write but should not have been at the expense of my past or my ancestral originality and heritage. An adequate blending of both ancient and modern education would have been superb! Don't you all think so? Bums!

The news of my going to live in the boarding house for my education saddened my grand-pa and his mates. They cried out because they saw that, my biological parents and their modern generation were not blending what had been valuable and timeless in their ancient tradition with their modern thoughts. Instead, they were doing everything possible to obliterate all that was ancient, timeless and traditional in their era. As wise men and women full of hard earned experiences and vision, they objected vehemently but, their era of family and village leadership was obviously over because they were in their 90s and growing weary and worn-out! They could only complain and watch and pray for God to show us a new light and overcome the evil ways consuming, pervading and overwhelming our rapidly growing generation. They knew we were lazy and running away from reality. They cried each time I was going back to the boarding house for social indoctrination in guise of social and better education.

For me as a child, I could not stop questioning, comparing and contrasting between my grand-pa's education which was direct and practical and my biological father's modern education which was distant and theoretical. I foresaw only a bleak future, felt hollow and started crying and knowing deep sadness at such an early age. It was truly depressing and devastating. Gradually, with the passage of time, deeper indoctrination and brain-washing through schools, I was forgetting all the nice and practical things that my grand-pa thought me. I was sort of officially brain-washed and with time I forgot the values of my grand-parents and their rich era.

As it was for me, so was it also for my fellow school mates. The authorities in charge of our modern education made sure they drilled and drained away any vestige of our past; (The teachers were only doing their best job, giving out what they had taken in); with time we started to think, dress, behave and act like them-(our appointed teachers and leaders). Finally, my country 'Nigeria' started to forget her ancestors and embrace other foreign cultures up till today with their little benefit and huge devastating repercussions.

Through our modern education we learnt mostly to: cheat fearlessly, armed robbery, forgery, drug-dependence in place of self dependence, betrayals and high level corruption. In my case, to further my education, I was whisked-off and jettisoned to a foreign country farther away from my grand-parents and his mates; away also from Nigeria and its abundant riches.

In abroad, far away from the comfort of home and security offered by parents, I was confronted with many challenges such as: the cultural differences, mental attitude of the host country, their different concept for things of creation etc. I was forced against my volition to confront: new language, new environment and constrained mobility against all legacies from my grandfather's generation; lack of

serious and worthwhile activities outside academic studies also bored the shit out of me and my colleagues most of the times.

As a result of all those confusions and frustrations being given by the authority in power, schools we attend and parents governed by absolute ignorance due mostly to insufficient experiences of life within and beyond them; consequently, in collaboration with my school mates we resorted to exam mal-practices, delinquency, drug consumption etc. Some of them also discovered what the world know as 'the popular '419' (advanced fee fraud) which today, as I write, is categorized as one of the biggest menace hindering and hampering the dignity and global respect for such a great nation as NIGERIA!

THE ORIGIN OF '419'- Advanced Fee Fraud-

Researching in my bid to know the origin of this popular '419' attached to my humble, intelligent, neglected and hardworking Nigerians abroad and home, I came up with a surprise finding in the 'Wikipedia.org! I read that the 'advanced fee scam' originated from the "Spanish prisoner" scam. There is a link at 'Wikipedia' that explains how '419' scam started in Nigeria in the 1980s.

Permit me to copy the information I read in 'Wikipedia' concerning this 'Advanced Fee Scam' for the benefit of those who have no access to the internet so they will know and understand that, Nigerian youth who have no job opportunities at home, because of shameful and gross corruption and mismanagement of their God-given resources; in their desperate bid to survive and live up to the expectations of their respective cultural and personal demands, use and apply recklessly, all means available and possible for them to earn a living and remain steadfast to their unbridled goals and aspirations – I must reiterate that, '419' or "advanced fee scam" is nothing to be proud of considering the nature of: economic, social, political and moral damages inflicted on other people by applying such fraudulent avenue for economic aggrandizement. Many times I have also fallen victim to that ghost and unseen monster! 'Advanced Fee Scam'

Below is Wikipedia trying to narrate the origin of '419' (Advance Fee Fraud)

"The Spanish Prisoner is a confidence trick dating back to the early 1900s. In its original form, the confidence man (con-man) tells his victim (the mark) that he is in correspondence with a wealthy person of high estate who has been imprisoned in Spain under a false identity. The alleged prisoner cannot reveal his identity without serious repercussions, and is relying on the confidence trickster to raise money to secure his release. The confidence trickster offers to let the victim supply some of the money, with

a promise that he will be rewarded generously when the prisoner returns; financially and perhaps also by being married to the prisoner's beautiful daughter. However, once the victim has turned over his money, he learns that further difficulties have arisen, requiring more money, and the trickster continues attempting to get more money until the victim is cleaned out and the process ends, presumably with the victim realizing he has been defrauded and that there is neither a rich man, nor a reward coming to him. Key features of the Spanish Prisoner trick are the emphasis on secrecy and the trust the confidence trickster is supposedly placing in the victim not to reveal the prisoner's identity or situation. The confidence trickster will often claim to have chosen the victim carefully, based on his reputation for honesty and straight dealing, and may appear to structure the deal so that the victim will distribute the confidence trickster's ultimate share of the reward voluntarily.

Modern variants of the Spanish Prisoner include the advance fee fraud, in particular the Nigerian money transfer fraud (or "419 fraud"). In the advance fee fraud, a valuable item must be ransomed from a warehouse, crooked customs agent, or lost baggage facility before the authorities or thieves recognize its value. In the Nigerian variation, a self-proclaimed relative of a deposed African dictator offers to transfer millions of ill-gotten dollars into the bank account of the victim in return for small initial payments to cover bribes and other expenses. More recent examples feature people sharing the same surname as the intended victim, with the scammer guessing the surname from observing patterns in email addresses, or obtaining full names from harvested email headers".

.

Though, some of my mates abroad remained steadfast to their studies and respective duties; they clinked to their studies with humility and dedication; adapted fully to the new and imposed cultural beliefs of their respective host countries. Those were the very ones trying to cleanse the bad notion of Nigerians as being corrupt to the core; crime infested and law-breakers. The Europeans and Americans in particular do not like to tolerate this class of people mostly for fear of inciting and inducing or awakening others into classical frauds and lawlessness. For that, they usually punish without remorse each time they get hold of anyone breaking their country laws or committing frauds of all categories!

From the above reference about the origin of 'Advanced Fee Fraud or Scam' let it be known that '419' or 'Advanced Fee Fraud' is not part of Nigerian culture or invention; it is rather, part and parcel of their studies abroad; part of the bad things they learn abroad as well as other positive things. I am not trying in any way whatsoever to support Nigerians, accept their nefarious and damaging engagements in Nigeria and abroad; but to rather "call a spade a spade", to put records straight for those who do not know the truth and facts of information they hear on daily basis. In addition, it will be pertinent to add that, from what I do know on face value about Nigerians, less than ten percent of the population is responsible for the bad image and name associated with the entire Nigerian citizens at home and in Diaspora. That is not a fair judgment or appropriate analysis of the facts on table; is it?

To solve a problem you must know the cause and source; knowing the source of each problem will help you to get faster to its root and then uproot it before it grows into a bigger tree with firm taproots. If for whatever reasons you are unable to detect the given problem on time before it had grown to a bigger tree full of branches and firm taproots, you then need some help to cut down the given tree.

The aim of this book is to bring that help which Nigeria nation will need to cut down its problematic tree which had continued to grow bigger with tap-roots and stronger branches in the passage of time. How do we begin this tedious job of salvaging a devastated Nigeria? Give your views please!

THE LEADERS AND LEADERSHIP IN NIGERIA

Nigeria as the great nation it has always been, amongst others, prides itself as one of the big nations where democratic mentality is prominent; in the very sense that anybody without exception, as long as you are a bona fide or proclaimed Nigerian citizen, can become a leader very easily in anyway, at all cost and at anytime.

 Nigeria as a great nation reserves the pleasure and privilege to accommodate three distinct systems of democratic government: **'military-democracy', 'democratic-democracy' and 'chieftaincy-democracy' or "traditional ruler ship".** As a great nation, true Nigerian citizens are so rich in mind, clever, strong and obsessively ambitious; so much is their respective ambitions that, anyone can wake up one day and decide to become the Nigerian leader and with little harassment here and there; if need be, with a bit of blood-shed or bribing one or two prominent persons, there you go as the "the honorable Excellency, the president of the federal republic of Nigeria". Why not?

 If you can be a president why can't I? "It is no one's inherited position or property"! That is the mindset and spirit of a true Nigerian man/woman. Such mental attitude also, symbolizes people with free minds; minds free from bondage as against ways things are seen in most advanced countries of the world where every step to reach any given position or activities remain conspicuously mapped-out. Somehow, the Nigerian system of government demonstrates such a positive attitude and spirit of enthusiastic, self esteemed, faithful and joyous people. This is the kind of spirit common among people full of self-confidence; the kind of mindset necessary for success and self realization.

Today, due to ignorance, uncertainty and lack of definite purpose or goal in the lives of Nigerian populace that untamed-spirit of freedom is globally portraying as: villains, law-breakers, cheats, thugs, fraudulent and corrupt people from a corrupt nation.

'Give us a break please; for we shall deliver well and remember- "he who laughs last, laughs best"!

That may surely sound ridiculous, clumsy and irrational for the elites with the big grammar who believe and live in the illusion that their system is the best. But, for radicals and liberal minded people like Nigerian youth from the post-seventies´ – their attitudes symbolizes such virtuous human traits which awakens: self-esteem, self-motivation, confidence and courage which average true Nigerian citizen carries along in them and transmits same to everyone within his or her immediate vicinity anytime and anywhere in the world. But, unfortunately, the majority of the aforementioned good human qualities seem to be more pronounced among the Igbo-Biafrans in Nigeria.

Those positive characteristics and many others are the fundamental reasons why Nigerians were voted as one of the happiest people in the world! Nigeria and Nigerians are not only and always "black and red" as the world tries to paint it/them. Trust me, the very day we Nigerians decide to rectify those little things holding us backwards such as: not keeping our streets and gutters clean, taking bribes and not doing an honest job in our duties; not accepting each other as one people with a common language for patriotism to foster; not electing only people with adequate requirements, appropriate characteristics and discernment to be at the helm of our national affairs etc. when we start doing those things right, Nigeria will surely become the 'apple of the world's eyes'. It will become the best nation on earth!

God, the creator; for whatever reason, has abundantly lavished blessings on the Nigerian nation: constant sunshine, regular rainfall, abundance of natural vegetation, few or nearly absence of natural disasters, excess of natural resources etcetera. Nigeria and other African countries have got more of Nature's blessings than they duly worked for. Africans should always jubilate loudly and gratefully than showing such senses of impotence and an under-privileged people! Why?

When you travel around the world and notice the much people have got to work, drill, and stress themselves before they could eat or own anything tangible to make them laugh and hopeful of tomorrow that must surely come, you will all understand the richness and abundances of all things in Nigeria as a nation. The same, for most African nations in where people work very less and eat very much, have nothing tangible and, still having the audacity to give away or share the little they could scoop from their rich soils. Where people have very minimum necessities for clothing, houses, security and heavy machinery in order to live and sustain themselves! Nigerians sing alleluia, Africans sings alleluia for the good Creator is in love with you. Your blessings are innumerable, so enjoy the glory in it! "The last shall become the first" it was written; do not forget that prediction in the timeless scripture!

Nigeria at fifty-Six years of independence as a sovereign nation has done well and bad comparatively. It had been governed for more period of time by the military than by the civilians but, whether the civilians or the military are in control of the government, the effect of the difference is usually barely noticeable by the citizens – thanks to the big sense of maturity crowning the rich heads of Nigerian people which is making it possible for them to adapt easily and go along nevertheless with: democracy by the civilians or democracy by the military; either of them is a foreign system of government: imported, borrowed and non-indigenous. Mistakes, uncertainties and confusions are normal to take place for a certain period of time. So, let's bury our hatchets, forgive one another, hope and wait for that day of absolute redemption! For now, in order to move forward, building and cultivating on fertile soils, it will be advisable to give more power and responsibilities to the traditional leaders for they represent and embody all or most of the legacies of our great ancestors. However, we need to sit down together as brothers /sisters to figure-out a system of leadership that will be most appropriate for Nigerian people, culture and geographical background.

TRADITIONAL LEADERS IN BIAFRA

-What is Traditional Leadership, and who make up the Traditional Leaders-?

Traditional leadership in the Biafran context is observing, knowing and following the customs and lifestyles of the ancestors through the mandate of an appointed person within a given region of the Biafran communities.

Traditional leaders are those people appointed by a given community, village or region to head their common affairs in relation to social, family, health, political and personal progress following and keeping the pathway of their past elders or ancestors.

What are the Criteria for Appointing a Traditional Leader in Biafra?

As I witnessed during the eras of my grandparents, traditional leadership is a privileged position offered to worthwhile indigenous sons of a given community with either special traits of character measured in the quality and dimension of knowledge, ability, determination and hard-work which had for one time or the other impacted the community in a positive way. With the passage of time, this noble position could be duly inherited. In the past, appointing community leaders was then based on strength, wisdom, empathy and an impeccable attitude and rectitude.

By whichever standard they may have based their choices however, in those days, most of the chiefs or traditional leaders were usually men of integrity, discernment, acting with honesty and the best interest of their kith and kin at heart.

Then traditional leaders in Biafra were very well known and they deeply understood the rudiments of medicinal herbs to cure their people of varying ailments; in their palms lay the history of their respective villages and beyond. They knew each family by name, origin and history. They were open and accessible to their subjects day and night, seven days a week (24/7) they were known in different regions of the Biafra land as Obis', Ezes' and Chiefs etc.

In those days, every indigenous person from any given community or region could feel and sense the unity and harmony between brothers and sisters of the same community; eating, playing, working and living together with love and affection! They mediated with utmost honesty and sincerity in all family and inter-tribal conflicts to the best of their abilities and knowledge without fear or favor. Their advice and guidance to their people were duly and respectfully accepted with joy and as an end to whichever issue that may have arisen! Such were the brief and common qualities of a traditional leader in Igbo land or entire Biafraland; the unadulterated legacies from our great ancestors.

Today, from the rising events of things, those ideals and criteria for appointing, choosing or inheriting community or tribal leadership titles are no more applied as was inherited; those virtuous characteristics for meritorious traditional leaders or chieftaincy title holders are being continuously politicized; its valor and value being scraped and badly manipulated. Surely, our ancestors will never be happy seeing or accepting such traditional leaders with little or no knowledge of the tradition or custom which they represent and embody.

The rules are changing towards a wrong direction; today, traditional leadership are given to those with more economic affluence or social influence apart from few regions who are still respecting the guidelines and system of rules and regulations inherited from their ancestors.

In reality, the Igbo ancestors related with their chiefs and leaders in optimum confidence and transparency. Their respected and trusted – Chiefs, Ezes and Obis or other leadership title holders were considered and seen as everything for the community: Herbal doctors, advisers, Judges, prophets etc. They were responsible for all forms of issues good or bad challenging or benefiting the community which they are entrusted with. They acted like good and loved fathers, uncles and brothers to the entire community without any sign or deeds based on prejudices; they were open and available to the entire citizens of the community twenty-four hours and seven days of the week; they never showed signs of disturbances than the prudent manifestation of wisdom, calmness and versatility. In a nutshell, the ancient Igbo chiefs and leaders, for their people, were the live- encyclopedia and the harbingers of all remote knowledge or history of the tribe or communities they represented; every dispute swiftly contained amicably with sisterly affection! Their women were allowed equal rights at a certain advanced age. Their women have equal or more contributions at any community or village meetings. Above the general village meetings involving the entire village: Men, women and youth, the women have their own separate associations which were organized solely by the married women of the village or kindred. In the similar way, the youth were allowed and encouraged to organize their own youth meetings and plan how to manage or confront any issues that may arise among them. The ancient Igbo-Biafra had observed a very complex and utter democratic system structure before the advent of colonialism and the amalgamated Nigeria nation which today remain our sovereign nation, although the center could not hold. I begin to wonder if it will ever hold based on the events of negative things surging and oozing out of every nook and cranny of the nation.

Traditional Religion in Igbo/Biafra

Those days during the era of our ancient people, our ancestors, their self-dependence and self-sustenance was total, complete and in absolute harmony with their indigenous: religion, government, agricultural techniques, building technique, food preservation technique, marketing, sports arenas and activities; music and cultural dancing techniques, medicine, marriages and everything humanly necessary to healthily rear and grow their inhabitants.

Ardent religious-minded-people and because of their freedom of choice and expression, nearly every kindred devised unique ways of manifesting and worshiping their divine concept of the Creator. Some referred to the Creator as: OLUWA in Yoruba, OSALOBUA in Edo, and CHINEKE or CHUKWU in Igbo etc. the only thing they did wrong according to our colonial masters was that, they applied the use of symbols to idolize divinity as they conceived it. They made animal and human sacrifices to God because they believed- that Chukwu or God deserved the best of everything for being mighty and mysterious. Whatever their crime and however it was committed, compared with today's people, with today's religion; I feel it is a gross injustice and outright negligence if history fails to recognize majority of the people of that era as Saints; and duly include their good names in the book of sainthood!

I cannot speak for others, but from my observations in their era and from what I know of history today and of then: I hereby declare my grand-pa, my grand-mamas' (Ikwuoma and Oyiridiya), my biological mother (Christiana), Amos Awo (our village chief) among others, as Saints! "Saint Obi", "Saint Ikwuoma", "Saint Amos Awo", "Saint Christina Obi" etc. among others are some of the forgotten and neglected personalities whom I happen to know from the last generation; yet, no one talks about them. Those were people without bad sins; honest humans.

So, how can the world be fair and successful if they fail to call a "spade a spade"? On this note, I will suggest that we have to rewrite the world history with sincerity and honesty – calling 'black as black' and 'white as white'. Until then the peace and harmony which we ardently seek, will continue to be elusive!

Today, the Christian and Muslim religion in Nigeria is becoming something else other than the real expression of gratitude and obeisance to the unseen and unique Creator as was meant to be. In places of worship, every day of the week, you will hear the deafening noises and shouting of supposed religious worshippers exorcizing, casting away and burning demons, witches and wizards. These days there is monetary value to everything. I used to wonder where all these innumerable groups of religious representatives were in the past before things went that far bad.

Today our country is saturated with men and women of God, prophets and pastors as well as places of worship. Question is: why these sudden surge of religious worshiping and worshippers? What went wrong with the religion and system of belief adopted and practiced byourr far and near ancestors? The Igbo/Biafra ancestors never practiced or had any pre-knowledge of: Christianity, Islam, Hindu or any other form of religion whatsoever. They simply respected the rules and dictates of their good conscience, shunning bad and ugly thoughts and deeds. They worshipped their God and their beliefs in Him personal and private, of which they expressed and manifested through gestures or with carved objects or images; Period! Religion for Igbo ancestors cannot go beyond self-conscience, belief and self-perception. Therefore, religion of all nature for the ancient Igbos was practiced mostly in private and then, sometimes with the statesmen and women of the community for some occasional offerings of thanksgiving or appeasement of their all potent God!

However, the modern Igbos should check and balance the spiritual inclination of our Godly citizens; and lead them towards the best possible pathway to God's knowledge which was divinely engraved deep-down-within each one of us from birth.

Blood Sacrifices

What is the essence of blood sacrifices to idols or otherwise; is it true or false that people do those things and if they do, what are the real benefits, how do such acts help to enhance our lives and achieve progress for our nation? Too much talk about voodoo, Juju, witches etc, as if all the negative and dark entities in life have taken our beloved people and country in perpetual ransom! Is it true, all the nasty occurrences we hear every day in relation to voodoo, witches and Juju? Because if those were true occurrences, I must confess my deep worries to see my entire country in this state of frenzy and deep fear of spiritual, economic and social insecurity and hopelessness. Biafran citizens and leaders must have to find a conducive and amicable balance over this disproportionate religious worshipping and practices endemic amongst my God-loving-people.

Nigeria/Biafra Film and Drama Industry

It is a thing of joy and pride to watch the rapid and progressive growth of the Nigerian film industry. This is a laudable avenue to create jobs for most youth with talent in acting and drama. It will help to increase the level of auto-esteem and self confidence in many youths' as well as providing medium of inspiration for most of them desiring to join the film business industry.

Obviously, the film industry ranks second after the News Media in creating visual and dramatic awareness of both the ills, progresses and intrinsic values of every given society.

However, apart from making money, providing jobs, creating awareness and becoming famous it will be worthwhile to alert our Nigerian Film Makers that: through the predominant casting of Juju or fetish acts and images in most of their films and drama; many Nigerians and all the neighboring countries have maintained the idea that – Nigerians and life in Nigeria is all based on 'Juju' and fetish practices. Through our many Voodoo or Juju films, most of our African neighbors had made the conclusions that, what they watch in the movies is synonymous to the real life in our country…

If you visit many countries today especially within African neighborhood, you will be embarrassed to know that – people are afraid to rent out their houses to you as a Nigerian for reasons ranging from: bad fetish concept seen in films, suspicion of fraudulent behaviors to any dimension – 419 (advanced fee fraud), robbery, cheating and 'Get-Rich-Quick Syndrome' which seems more notorious and predominant among my Nigerian people.

Films can be a very conducive avenue to mitigate and neutralize such erroneous beliefs of most people around the world. It can be used to re-educate and bring back dignity to and confidence in the Nigerian populace both in and beyond Nigerian boarders.

We can use or apply the influence and popularity of the film industry to bring more respect and global acceptance for Nigeria through casting and producing positive oriented movies and dialogue.

Surely, most of the films are great and near or equal in all standards, no doubt; but majority of the films are notwithstanding, busy portraying the image of Nigeria solely based on betrayals, cheating and fetishes'. Of course, Nigerians are not just only fetish; we are and do lots of other nice things than Juju, cheating and betraying one another at all time and at all cost! That impression will not be fair to millions of innocent, disciplined, God-fearing and loving Nigerians.

The government should also try to be able to censor the kind of images of the country that are being portrayed and disseminated to homes and foreign public through Media information. That should be a part and parcel of the governments' duties; to conduct and regulate all national affairs, issues and activities concerning Nigerian citizens in and out of the country.

The Nollywood Film Industry at the present is composed in majority of the Igbos or the Biafran indigenous people; *if Biafra separates out of the present Nigeria, what shall the fate of Nollywood be? Will the Nollywood continue to function as a united Film Industry – of which I see no reason why it should not continue-... or will it be affected negatively by the prospect of the Igbos' separation out from Nigeria?*

Whatever the outcome, my advice for caution still stands firm and true for Nigerian, Biafran or even any other African country...As actors, you must bear in mind that your profession is one of the best avenues to inform, educate and awaken the public on the looming realities of life and ways of living our given lives in real time. Use this chance to positively impact and impart on any of your audience. Let people know the beauty, wealth and humane lifestyle of the African people and their continent. You are in the best position to positively rewrite the tainted and dented image of Africa and Africans at large. Keep keeping up the good work!

MODERN BIAFRAN LIFESTYLE

– Village to City and City to the Village-

In Biafra, it had gradually become an unwritten culture or lifestyle for people to move from the villages where they were born and retain automatic right to lands and properties, to the cities where there are modern amenities for studies, schools and administrative or 'white-collar-jobs'. This is not a very relevant topic. It serves only to make my beloved Biafrans and Africans in general to know and understand how rich their lands and lives are in the natural sense of facts.

In Europe, America and most advanced countries, people have no memory or knowledge of what their ancestral homes were like due to sustained periods of wars which marked their formative years and high rate of rapid structural/technological development. Their system is organized in such a way that every bona fide citizen should begin to make one income or the other, in return, begin to pay taxes to the government till retirement (which is usually after 40-50 years of constant work in any field of endeavor) Of course, with one month holiday within every 12 calendar year to be in a position to pay taxes to the protecting government! in the advanced nations, when you are paying taxes, then you have right to ask and obtain some of the enticing benefits which the government voluntarily makes available to induce people to keep, obey and maintain "laws and orders" such benefits include: health care, social assistance for children between 1 to 18 years of age; retirement allowances and assistance to those who are unemployed etc. This is generally, the system of things in the technologically advanced countries.

This kind of system of government, as good as it sounds and as protective as it may be, has got its disadvantages too. For all those benefits, assistances and excessive controls make life "super-monotonous" and boring for most people in the said technologically advanced nations; leading to depressive conditions which, in turn results in lack of enthusiasm among majority of the citizens. These are major weights crowning all heads in every "advanced nations of the world". Those are the price-tags one should pay in order to avail of the benefits in their respective societies of residence as in all things of God and of man.

Contrarily, in Nigeria or for Biafrans, the situation is more personalized. The government does not have a system permitting every citizen to work and pay taxes to them which should justly be used for the citizens-welfare. Instead, out of their own volition citizens choose to pay tithe to: churches, thugs, and indigenous community contributions for protection and assistance which will be given strictly in times of needs. They have the freedom to manage their own things in their own ways, when and wherever they deem fit.

Unlike the advanced countries, Biafrans do not need to become experts in any given field to start their own businesses to any level their imagination could carry them. Unlike the advanced countries, Biafrans do not need to work for three-sixty-five days that make up a year with just thirty days holiday in between and do not need to search for a place or country with adequate sunshine and warm sea to spend few weeks-holiday; because they still have their ancestral homes intact: full of natural vegetation, warm and relaxing.

Due to such rich advantages available for them, people prefer to go back to their villages from the hustle and bustle of the City life without the real need to go any farther to search for leisure, rest and relaxation. It is obvious from those little differences to grasp the abundant richness of the Biafran land, people and culture.

Therefore, my advice here should be that: the Biafran system by all means, should as a matter of urgency devise ways to regularly assist its citizens in upgrading the standard of living conditions in the villages through providing: steady electricity, clean water, medical and sanitary facilities to enable those living in those villages to be able to live comfortably as well as being able to retain and maintain the legacies and glories of their past without abandonment. Doing so will surely motivate the youth of the families living in distant cities to go home regularly and find a way to enhance the real rural development projects and to prevent the frequent mass youth exodus; those are some of the best approach to consolidate the nucleus of any technological foundation prior to its further advancement.

The real technological know-how is based on cultural concepts and beliefs which are then carried out into action and molded into monumental edifices that can enhance and nourish the peoples' concept and creative genius or potentials; of which, will then become the beacon from which posterity will appraise, appreciate and continue to grow or advance from there towards the far future! At the end of the day, "charity must begin from home to be authentic"

It is my utmost belief that, if we could all find a way to put the best interest of the Biafran people into perspective, motivating everyone to give their best also in services for better future for all, surely, such move will definitely enhance a sense of patriotism among rulers and citizens; which will induce them to do their best with love and humility. These are the only things lacking to put Igbo/Biafrans in their rightful place in the global affairs. True patriotism, proactive and sustainable goal carried out under the good spirit of utmost sincerity and high sense of patriotism; those are all we need and ask for in order to better ourselves and take

charge and control of out near and far future; the rest we have gotten them in

abundance, thanks to Chukwu Okike Abiama!

PART 4

LOOMING BIAFRA & NIGERIA CHALLENGES - *Possible Solution-*

In Biafra land like in most parts of the world, especially in Africa, the first and most devastating problems draining and drowning the entire citizens are: "abject ignorance", superstition, and lack of educational system designed in harmonious relationship with the universal principles of life and living; designed to embrace the culture, language and above all, the general perception of this world and beyond by the entire citizenry.

Ignorance is a normal human characteristic which simply means: "having little or no knowledge" of oneself, situations around and beyond the individual or entire community. And no one can pride of knowing everything; therefore, we are all ignorant of one thing or the other. Knowledge and wisdom is our divine task; nature has it that we must know, we should know through: learning, actions, experiences, observation, analysis, imaginations and subtle inspirations. Even, as humans replete with such an alarming level of ignorance, our society still encourages that we must learn to know either by force or through persuasion.

To back-up such convictions, we came up with such expressions as "ignorance is not an excuse for not knowing the laws". If we should accept that notion, and seeing the high level of ignorance in our respective countries and the world from the past to present day, we must have to admit the stack fact that we are having serious challenges in our hands that require prudent handling.

A person who understands enough of him or herself will naturally know that he or she will never know all the intricacies and infinite mystery of this world– knowing is conceiving and experiencing things and putting them into test through realistic actions.

And this is where: honesty, humility, faith and determination come into play in our lives. Without those fundamental principles obtainable through self-discipline, caution and positive mental attitude, ignorance will continue to devour our minds and souls like cancer by hindering all sources of knowledge and wisdom.

In Biafra as or in Nigeria, instead of putting the little we do know into self and national development, we rather choose short-cuts to avoid the real hard-work required for things to be done and done well; ignorance is an inherited sickness which we are meant to overcome and triumph over within the track of our individual lives. To know beyond the extraordinary is our divine obligation.

Therefore, to treat any kind of sickness we must first diagnose and dissect the problems in order to find the cause before a possible solution can be administered. And when you have ascertained the cause, you will then prescribe and give treatment with the high faith that your prescribed treatment permanently or partially cures the sickness. In the same way we have tried to diagnose Nigeria & Biafra as patients; now let's see about cure.

Below are listed some of the major problems or challenges inflicting the minds of Nigeria citizens that is making all laudable intent to progress, proactive and effective national development in the entire country very difficult to perpetuate:

- lack of patriotism
- corruption
- abundance of natural resources
- lack of a uniform language
- neglect of rural areas and people
- lack of a uniform cultural background from the ancestors

- superstitions and wrong ancestral values

- Absence of a documented history of the past before, during and after the colonial influences over these geopolitical regions known as Nigeria.

For Nigeria or Biafra to ride in the wagon of: economic, social, political and technological development, She must positively address the above issues. Let us try to expatiate the above topics one after the other:

A: - Lack of Patriotism among Leaders & Citizens

What then is patriotism?

Patriotism is giving and showing one's unreserved loyalty and services to one's own country.

How many of you give and show your unreserved loyalty and services to your sovereign States or countries?

The fact here is that, 'patriotism' is not a tangible item, therefore, a mind-issue; it is a choice-concept; you may choose to be or not to be patriotic without any issue. Like yourself, your family and things of appreciation, your country should be accepted in the same vein for true sense of patriotism to foster and perpetuate for long in any citizen of any given country.

But, to inculcate the sense of patriotism into the mindset of citizens of any given country, the said country itself, must in similar vein practice giving to its citizens in abundance; this complies with the Golden-Rule' of Creation. You must give enough and established facts to people before you can voluntarily and involuntarily receive their loyalty and devotion; you must win their confidence; the unreserved confidence of the country's citizens to earn their respect and loyalty, for patriotism to soar.

If you can start today to give and wait to receive tomorrow, things will naturally improve on the positive path for Biafra or for and her neighbors within the gradual progress of time! Being patriotic is synonymous with being grateful and appreciative of where you are, what you receive out of the place you are and above all, how much are you contributing for the gradual and smooth functioning of where you are now-country.

B:- Corruption

Corruption in this context is obviously the opposite of patriotism. Like being loyal and respectful to someone or something, you do not think of doing harmful things to that person or thing, knowingly. Most of the time also, people are pushed to corrupt practices due to certain human factors as: greed, selfishness, fear of lack, sickness and death. Basically, all humans have such instincts as part of their character traits.

Corruption is never limited to any unique nation or race of people; it is part and parcel of human nature. Like other negative traits or vices endemic amongst human-race, corrupt attitude or traits can be curbed and reversed for honest services that will be more beneficial to all people on a national and international perspective.

However, you must all know that, corrupt practices are the major set-back in the Nigerian system of government. Corruption and corrupt practices are holding my beloved country at ransom without a foreseeable easy way out. What are our chances of overcoming corrupt practices and to move our dear country NIGERIA' forward? We shall duel upon ways to curb or minimize corrupt practices as we proceed deeper inside this book.

C: - Abundance of Natural Resources in the Country

Biafra as an ancient sovereign region had and still do have too much of everything; too much of man-power and of natural resources! Spoilt-Children! That is what Biafrans are; 'Spoilt-Children'. God the Father did spoil them all by giving too much of everything to us: regular Sunshine all year round, steady rainfall, high humidity conducive for plant vivacity. How can you imagine and enumerate the abundant number of natural resources waiting to be tapped and utilized for citizen's wellbeing; simply, too much to quantify the abundant resources in Biafra and the rest regions around and beyond the Nigeria boarders.

Why then do you over labor and suffer for what you already have? That is human Nature; let us blame such wrong choices and actions governed by obvious ignorance as 'being the other side of human coin', nature has it that, if you have got so much of anything whatsoever, you won't have the immediate need to think of the future of that which you already had with little sweat. You take the common gifts or life components for granted and therefore, living in the present without appreciation, accountability and responsibility and above all, aimlessly. People commonly act in that way when they have most things of life sorted for them...

Nothing is permanent; the world circulates like a running vehicle; every created thing is bound for change; change is the only permanent thing that cannot vary. You should therefore not take your lives and environments for granted.

You and your environment will change with time whether you understand the fact that you should always give and have the best in return or not.

Don't limit yourselves as you do by just: praying, asking and worshipping your traditional and religious God/s; good thoughts and deeds speak louder and give back in return more than you will ever gain from only asking and begging.

Don't suppress your good heart desires for positive changes; listen attentively to your heart and choose to follow only the positive route for change; with time and in faith your problems will be more than half solved.

To live and move forward in economic and social security, Biafrans like the rest of the African countries must learn to practice preservation methods so as to enable them cultivate food items in surplus; and the surplus can be preserved and reserved against periods when the plants and crops from farms go into recess; this preservation method will help to keep such food items in the markets for the public to continue to enjoy the said foodstuff long after harvest.

Further step will be to be able to export some of the excess produce for economic reward for national infrastructural development.

If we actually understand the fact that: everything in this globe we call Earth' is embedded underneath, deep-down-within the 'Earth's Belly'; in which many creatures live and survive such as: worms, certain rodents and microbes; while human creatures, plants and other animals live and survive on the earth-surface.

There exists also, differences in the types of soil or land structure found in different parts of the earth or world as you may choose to call it; some surfaces of earth areas are duly covered by ice, some covered by rocks only, some good portion covered by water, some covered by sand all across the area and very few places covered by forest or soil with trees and grasses etc. it has been ascertained by humans in the course of time or history that, the best soil component most conducive for human and other creatures to inhabit is found in those portions of the earth covered by thick vegetation. Biafra is among the lucky nations with very conducive soil component that is excellent for cultivation of nearly all types of food crops, fruits, animals etc. Besides all such divine blessings, Biafra is still not self-sufficient in food production; is she? The same bleak situation for Nigeria and most of the other African countries with equally good soil components, yet, they are not able to produce enough food from the fertile soil naturally given to them; **are they? And why are they not?** Because of lack of focus or long term vision; just as simple reason as that, my people are hungry, unhappy and perishing in abyss!

Every other thing is freely given by mother-nature; the rest depends on our individual or national need and use of those things already given to us by the Creator! We will sit down and plan the best way to use our given resources to live well and good enough. The Creator is always happy when His little creatures are living happily and merrily. This book will help to arouse massive national awareness to the best practices to achieve: self, regional and national development on the positive path. We must as matter of necessities adjusts our mental attitudes towards things of creation in a way that should enhance and foster patriotism, humility and sense of responsibility to achieve peace and harmony. Pray for that!

D: - Neglect of Rural Regions in Biafraland

Based on my trips across many horizons without end around the globe, I discovered that 'Money' is the worst of all inventions made by humanity; because of money and easy access to it, many healthy and strong youths recklessly abandon their rural areas in search of easy money in other distant places. There are all levels of these kinds of migrations; some chose to leave their place of birth to bigger cities; others travel abroad for the same ill-justified reason – **'money'**.

The above trend is indirectly causing a lot of damage to those living in such regions and their environment in the following ways:

- Rural neglect and abandonment of your place of birth, your father's house and property to travel abroad or to the big city in your country, either way, means that you are denying your manpower to the expansion and development of your father's property or your very rural heritage; also, by so doing, without knowing it, you are directly depriving yourself of the: knowledge, wisdom and cosmic energy or habit-force that unites you with your very place of birth and parental influence. Simply put, you lose contact with your originality and that cosmic energy or habit-force with which you were delivered into the womb or garden of this 'Mother-Earth'.

- you can notice, each time you go to a new place or country, you have to start all over to readapt to the new environment; sometimes, such adaptation takes longer for some, for others it may be a traumatic experience; and many never ever try to leave their birth places out of fear of having to start all over to learn to live in a new place. These are normal and acceptable human traits, because, nature's law has it that: 'human race and in fact all creatures will always desire things which are farther away out of their reach; that is the meaning of 'continuity and infinity', that sensation is what give humans the drive to move on with life and its constant inclemency and deep emotions or rise and fall; ebb and tide. It's all fine. The important thing is to be aware and understand those cosmic-habit-force or pattern of things of the universe.

Now, in Biafra as in many other regions of the world, because of money and desire for fame and power, instead of combining their youthful manpower and ideas to

build their respective places of birth, starting from where their ancestors stopped and gradually grow and better, they will instead prefer to abandon all that for a shorter-cut for money in other areas of the world while their father's property remain fallow, sequestered by stubborn weed and wretched from long neglect.

For this same money and the confusions it carries with it, you will find a Biafran in every nook and cranny of this world in search of quick and fast money. Some are living well even in Eskimos, some are in prison and others are stranded in the streets begging for alms and so on, the same goes for most youth from other areas of the world.

The same thing is happening in all the major cities of Nigeria, especially Lagos City; are you all aware of the gross insecurity engulfing our beloved nation or not? These things have some psychological impacts, you cannot blame the youth or the children for their gross misconduct and indiscipline; such blames should rightly go to the parents, and our ancestors; because it is usually from the fruit, that we can know the very tree that produced that very fruit…

We are not trading blames; I want to see my country progress on a positive, durable and fruitful trend with the understanding of the cosmic habit-force of creation.

Let us all forgo excessive superstitions, praying and just begging for miracles; instead, let's practice more working and giving so as to keep our minds very busy to have time for devil's works deep within us.

Based on all of the above unpleasant issues, I have structured one of the most viable possibilities to recoup and revamp our Biafra as a groovy and vibrant region instead of an infested and scornful area and people.

What the hell! Biafrans got talent', energy, manpower, natural resources and great men and women, so let's start to work now for good in order to enjoy later rewards. "Let us make haste while the sun is shining"

I will explain how to begin again at the last pages of this book, so read on! No shaking! We must make it to the top!

E: - Absence of a Precise Documented Ancestral History

There are no written guidelines, rules, regulations or references of the true lifestyles and achievements of our Igbo ancestors. There was no recorded history by them, no concrete written legacy left behind for their posterity and as a result, we had to grow in abject ignorance of our ancestors and their past. Because of that inherited ignorance, we continue to toil and struggle for a better life without a definite purpose or focused goal ahead of or awaiting for us.

The biggest crime of our Nigeria or Biafra ancestors which obviously continue to hunt us today was that idea of handing over all their doctrine and their cultural heritage which binding them together, just by the words of mouth;, and which will be destined to perish or misinterpreted at the death of the individual who inherited the cultural principles of the said community or race.

The stark truth is that, our ancestors had a life, a wonderful lifestyle indeed. The only omission was their inability, for whatever reason, to device writing or calligraphic and reading techniques which would have helped them to: narrate, document and propagate their myriad activities and laudable achievements in their relentless efforts to survive and live, be it in peace or at war alongside the unpredictability of the entire nature. Their ability to live in harmony with nature as it was presented to them was a commendable and laudable feat which we as their offspring, find very hard today to cope with;

instead, we foolishly harm, vandalize and thwart the set-down natural sequence of the things of creation. This is one of the major problems confronting the entire Nigeria and the rest of the African continent. To correct this, we should sit together and devise a feasible way to begin to outline, document and bind our ancestral heritages as purely as we witnessed them. Then disseminate and make such knowledge available for rapidly growing children as done by other well established countries or continents of this world. That will help the growing youth to know their history, mindset, and general perception of their ancestors…

F: - Lack of Inherited or Structured Common National Language

Obviously, Nigeria has always been a nation under orchestrated treachery and divergence. From the little I know about Nigeria's history, I learnt that it was the colonial masters who joined or amalgamated the different culture, language and geographical zones into one governable entity in order to have what we today call 'Nigeria'; fine, there is nothing wrong with that action itself for merging the people from the North, East , West and South to form a united Nigeria; thanks to them, the British; we today have a great nation with the highest population, manpower and rich natural resources in the whole of the African continent! This act on itself should not be an important issue in my personal views.

The main issue here is the very idea to merge tree major ethnic races together and govern them as one nation – the Yorubas, the Hausas and the Igbos and other minor ethnic groups- that 1914 obnoxious idea by Lugard to amalgamate the people of these divers regions still lingers today as one of the major factors hindering and hampering real peace, unity and harmony in every facet of political, economical, educational, technological and cultural ventures in this contraption – Nigeria- and beyond since after the country's independence from the British colonialist.

Why did it not work?

-Languages are naturally compiled based on personal experiences or concept of certain genealogy out of long years of wandering around the world or long occupation of a region; --language is a form of cultural expression and representation that manifests how a certain group of people in the beginning conceived, lived and manifested their general communal lifestyle at a point in time-space-continuum.

-Peoples' true intrinsic identity as a language is usually conceived and embedded in the core of their physical and psychological expressions at all moments-

'Peoples' ancestral language is a mirror reflection of their culture and total beliefs in the general framework of the world and life'; that is why the amalgamation is far from working!

That is to say that, the words people or communities use to represent whatever they see or imagine within their respective vicinities at any given time of their lives, show their core mindset and what we term as cultural heritages. The heritages are what guide and abide those groups of people during that moment of time; through imagination, association and comparing out of which words were usually invented, transmitted and accepted; listing the names of things as they are conceived. These are some of the most logical ways that races and their communities derive their words which they speak and names for things they use under the umbrella of creation.

Those are how cultural beliefs and backgrounds are founded; these are among others, how languages are determined and generally accepted and spoken. If these analyses are accepted to be facts of humans, and in the Nigerian context as a sovereign nation, is that part of her success story? Big NO! Nigeria is not an ancient name or place which is the very reason today Nigeria nation do not has a uniform or common language.

Therefore, to unite Nigeria as a sovereign nation, we must first concentrate on formulating a uniform language which all Nigerian citizens will be able to speak whether they are attending to school or not; whether educated or not; and in addition to whatever their spoken dialects from their places of birth and growth had been! This will be the first step in the bid to unite Nigeria and imbibe into her citizenry an unshakeable sense of patriotism and belonging!

How shall we formulate a common language at this stage for all Nigerians?

No doubt, structuring a common language for Nigeria at this stage of life and growth seems nearly impossible. It poses clearly a herculean task but, very easy to achieve with a clear-cut- vision and mission spread along the distant future with persistence, determination and national agreement or cohesion! I have designed a feasible project to achieve this which you will read at the end of this book. And that is in the case that, we all continue to remain inside Nigeria as one indivisible nation; alternatively, separate the amalgamated regions back as they were before Nigeria- was proclaimed and each region should rule themselves according to the use of a common language; and, or nullify and reconsider the 1914 Lord Lugard Amalgamation act which brought us forcefully together!

G: - Superstition and Wrong Ancestral Values

It is evident from the trend of things in Nigeria society and the mental attitude of most Nigerians that superstition and wrong ancestral values are among others one of the most devastating factors hindering and slowing-down proactive progresses in the entire nation of Nigeria.

The formative years of any human being are the most critical period especially, from year 01- 08 which, had been accepted around the world as the most effective period for children education. This is a very fundamental stage when the right or wrong information is being transmitted and inculcated into the **'Brain-Chip'** of every individual…. (You will read more on that in my next book **'How to Educate Children with Ease'**) in that book you will see that children actually begin gradually and unconsciously to learn or assimilate information from the very day they were born and from then on increase their rate of reasoning and assimilation of information from between two to six years of age. By the time children are approaching ten years of age, they are full adults by natural sequence; you can notice the rapidity of their imagination, curiosity, endless questions, high pitched energy force etc. On your own, you can observe the natural ability to think and reason well as adults do.

Now, in the world as a whole, from my trips across the horizon, I discovered that **most of the problems in the world are man-made.** I realized that majority of the parents in this world have got no clue on the sound and appropriate ways to bring up a child without making a lot of mistakes- and by giving the correct information about all things to the best of their knowledge as parents-

Now in the Nigerian context, we are not free from the same error as above; without much concentration, you can easily see that Nigerians are among the worst parents I have ever known in all these years of my shuttling around the world. Why? Because in my beloved country, our parents start to shout and kick the 'living-organs' out of us even from the first one month of our birth on Earth- hahaha; As a child, they will shout on you with all their anger and frustration with life; they will shout and kick your ass with equal ferocity as if you are the devil incarnate yourself or part of the problem in their lives; they will call you some ugly names that make you wonder if that is a joke or for real…even at schools, a teacher comes into a class and start to flog all the children in his or her class because they are making noise, or playing etc. there is no room for dialogue. All such approach to children education are wrong and unfruitful, it's hard to make a good human through intimidation and castigation, such actions are duly loaded with high level negative psychological impact on growing children; and even, more on when they become full adults.

On the other hand, your father will continue to encourage you to be material rich, your mother will tell you to marry a rich person with money, houses, cars and fashion; these are the main ambitions our parents have been deeply inculcated and imparted into us right from when we were children.

What do you think will happen to a child full with such negative information about life?

In Nigeria or Biafra, growing up as children, no one taught us how to plan for the future, adventure, discover and document; how to keep our minds positive and clean of rut and negative thoughts etc.

Our ancestors were busy practicing and teaching witchcraft, building fear and making sacrifices to idols without time to teach their children real-life-issues which shall be bound to impart positive and balanced progress.

Those are some of the major problems in the Nigeria society as I sit writing; I repeat, Biafrans on one-to-one, are among the best human-beings I have had the fortune to know in my entire life. They have a very rich background but with wrong information in their brain-chip right from the beginning- those negative forces are what is wrong with the average Nigerian or Biafran…do not ever blame my people because they are doing the best in their abilities with what they were given growing as birthright.

When we know or discover our problem, the solution become easier; from now onwards try to transmit the correct information on real life issues to our growing children; in this way going, the growing youth will be able to correct the errors of the past and to make the present and the future better than today!

How to enhance durable self and national development in Biafra/Nigeria

For any nation to move forward in the positive and right direction, all of the negative factors which we have being discussing from the start of this book, have got to be appropriately and sincerely addressed through devising long lasting solutions to most of those inherent and acquired problems or challenges. *That can only be done beginning with love for ourselves, neighbors and unrelenting patriotism for our nation in general.*

How do we then ensemble and propagate that missing sense of patriotism in all Nigerian/ Biafran?

The easiest way to capture, cultivate and imbibe a laudable sense of patriotism into the minds of the general public will have to be through:

PART 5

Leadership by Example

What is leadership?

Leadership simply means: headship; to be on the lead, to be the first to do; to serve others with what you know better than them; experienced and conversant with the way, so that you can dutifully lead others through in the same pathway leading to good deeds and self realization. That is my definition and concept of the word 'LEADERSHIP'

Meaning that, those elected to lead others should try against all odds to practice what they preach. We are not asking for total honesty among the leadership hierarchy because it is abnormal not to have opposing and challenging factors in your ways as you travel along this journey for life and of living.

If our elected leaders could have among them about forty against sixty percent (40-60 %) of non-corrupt leaders at the helm of our national affairs, the positive impact from the 40% will be stronger and more compelling than the remaining 60% of corrupt leaders. **Because, as a rule of nature – good deeds always win over evil deeds on the long-run! Thanks to the Omni-potent Creator!** This is not for Biafran or Nigerian leaders alone but, referring to the global community leadership mindset in general:-

-You cannot preach peace to win the confidence of your people while your real or ulterior motive is mischief or war.

-You cannot stand in front of the expectant, confused and frustrated citizens' who are earnestly searching for deliverance, and preach to them: discipline, unity and justice while behind your mind; embezzlement and deceit is your ulterior motive. You can act and do as you please with yourselves when your time comes for decision making and action taking; but, know it that every single decision and action you take is duly recorded in your 'brain-chip' and the credits and debits are as well duly yours at the time to   reckon. Cheating, hurting and intimidating others are lousy kind of low-lifestyle. Fear, greed and materialism are the chief causes of wickedness and heartless devastation of other people's lives and properties; or, and the infringement of peoples' birthright to live within the divine rule of their conscience embedded deep down within them.

Know also, that every secret action you take must always come to light in accordance with nature's laws. There is no hiding place; because all existing things are intricately intertwined; only a question of time for the tide and current to get to you wherever you may be.

-Let it also be known to you that it is pure ignorance that induces men to err and err again; for if you could be persistent enough to understand the principles and subtle nature of creation, the meaning of 'habit-*force*' or *pattern of cosmic things, people then must be willing to think and act positively; for when you come face to face with the truth and lingering heart wrecking repercussions of wrongdoings, surely, you will understand how simple and safe it is to do good than bad.*

-Let it also be known to you that you must *pay or benefit from everything you do in direct proportion to the intensity of joy or pain given out to or from others; so, in reality you don't do anything for no one but for yourself. Whatever you think, decide and do is for you alone. Fundamentally, everything you ever did or will still do is or are done but, for yourself alone; in the same order you will receive the credit or debit for all your deeds; such is one of Natures' basic laws. "To be warned is to be armed" stop cheating and betraying each other, such deeds cause self and collective frustration; and then, if not abated shall result in self or collective damnation.*

The Spirit of Patriotism

The good spirit of patriotism, if and when achieved and infused in the bloodstream of the citizens of any country, will surely induce and motivate the majority of the masses in such given countries to do positive deeds like: keeping our streets and gutters clean; most people consciously doing their respective jobs with diligence, honesty, drive and imagination. That same spirit of enthusiasm will also induce more government officials to shift their efforts from wrong to doing what is just and right; spirit of patriotism will ginger leaders to act with compassion and provide basic amenities: electricity, clean water, good roads, Medicare facilities, insurance against loses, pension scheme for all their citizens! In our own context as Nigerians or Biafrans, what makes us a rich nation if our indigenes can´t benefit from those basic and natural amenities due to them by the natural privilege of birth?

Spirit of patriotism especially when practiced by those on the echelon of leadership, will naturally induce the citizens of that nation, to readily give out all their best energy, for selfless services to their beloved nation and inhabitants with utmost enthusiasm; while they nourish in the deep subtle pleasure that rewards every good deed.

For any country to be sovereign should naturally have a common inherited spoken language that all its citizens should be able to understand and speak fluently, even without having previously attended the four walls of an academic institution; Period!

A race is carved out of the language they speak; and the language a race speaks makes them an indigenous race.

The subtle natural joy for giving and sharing should be the ulterior spiritual pursuits of every human entrusted with the divine duty to oversee the sacred Mantle of peoples' leadership or headship.

Nevertheless, like in all things of this life that are worth having, they should be worth working for as well' – if you desire patriotic citizens, you must be able to cultivate patriotism and be patriotic enough yourself in the first place. That is all it naturally takes to motivate and induce people to willingly follow you to work without reservations; that is the only valid code to win peoples' confidence on a long term basis.

There are no magic sticks or wand to doing things right and well other than through thought, decision and action sequence in the full absence of bias or prejudice. Whenever dealing with people: your children, wife, friends, and communities; upwards to your nation and the world in general, once in your mind, bias or prejudice sets in while dealing with people, your results and ingathering at the long run, will never be complete or fulfilled...divine cosmic rules!

If you don´t know thyself, you can´t guide thyself nor know or guide others. And in absolute terms, how many of us know ourselves well enough as to know and lead others?

Leadership in literal definition should mean- unanimous peoples´ choice after analyzing, deciding and come to choose one of their sons or daughters to head or lead them to prosperity, health and happiness. Choices of electing or appointing a leader in any given establishment are always based on people´s convictions of the chosen person´s-wisdom, integrity and fairness entrusted in faith that he or she shall deliver them and their collective expectations.

In real times, without leadership coherence with the people's initial expectations, the leader can't lead the people to achieve of their natural heart desires.

When you lead people without knowing thyself' you can't anticipate and comprehend the people's needs and aspirations in an unequivocal term. Your leadership is headed to fail because you are not ruling in line with inherited natural law of conscience; the "birth-rule". At this height, the only chance left to continue leading people will be through orchestrated lies, intimidation, and hypocrisy to pacify and encourage the people to continue to follow you even without their volition... is this last not the politics of These Days?

Leaders who cannot deliver their promises to their people they lead what next will they expect in return? – Strife, lack of confidence and chaos; and when those begin to happen, the leaders will resort to lies, patching up of holes created along trailing on the wrong pathway. In due course, the people will awaken to the lies and deceit; what happens next?

Whenever you see those signs in any community, it means that the incumbent leadership is simply not living up to the people's expectations; because, it is naturally impossible to live to peoples' expectations, therefore, impossible to rule people to achieve prosperity and growth bound in peace, unity and harmony through all structured and orchestrated modern leadership ensemble.

For peace's sake, now is time of awakening and due for us to sit back, review and reshuffle our leadership terms and conditions, not only for Nigeria or Biafra but, for the entire globally established system of people and business governance.

In essence, regrettably, it is obvious that humans are having hard work to accumulate enough wisdom necessary to embark on political legislation structured to bring lasting solution, unity, wealth and harmony among themselves as specie.

The best way to achieve a better governance is to make rules that will be enshrined, streamlined and deeply anchored within the precincts of the "Universal Rules" or the "Golden Rules" of nature; the "Rule of the Conscience" "The Birth-Rule"…

In essence, what do we want precisely out of life?

If we peace for example, we should strive to know the line of rules that will definitely head towards achieving that peace going for next decades…

If unity is what we want, there sets of rules that are bound to lead to that going for decades…but, today, in nearly all over the Planet earth, in place of unity, peace and harmony what we have instead are discord, disunity, and disharmony; why so? - Our leadership orientation and foundation are wrongly interpreted and disseminated. Time for change back to nature's rule for unit and peace to reign once in our life time!

THE NIGERIA/BIAFRA CIVIL WAR (*6th July 1967-15th January 1970*)

(Author's Childhood Narrative of His Personal Experiences during and after the war)

During this war period, there was a state of total unrest and uncertainty looming around every part of Nigeria as a sovereign nation. The situation was reflected in the ways of the people, especially parents, were doing things with obvious uncertainties and doubts; they were consciously attached to the multi-band transistor radios (one of the legacies of the colonial masters) in a desperate bid to know what was going on in the seat of government. As a child of barely five years of age, I was aware that something was seriously wrong with our country: the groups of women gossiping, students, illiterate and children who were analphabet and were repeating the daily rumors they overheard from their parents; everyone with different versions of the actual situations.

In those days, there weren't adequate media information except through little transistor radios owned by just a few individuals in a whole city and maybe one or two 'black and white TV' sets found in sporadic families—mostly families of those who had worked with or been in some kind of contact with the colonial men and women. During the same period, I was whisked away from Ugbelle, my birthplace by one of my uncles and to the city of Enugu to stay with him along with a niece and my older sister.

Nearly eight weeks after I left my village Ugbelle and arrived in Enugu, the rumors of a civil uprising from the capital city- Lagos State- had been on the increase with more frightening and tangible consequences. Headed by Lft. Colonel Chukwuemeka Odumegwu Ojukwu, the eastern region of Nigeria was demanding for separation from the Nigerian government in order to form an independent government of their own as 'Federal Republic of Biafra' with the sovereign rights of a country. Consequent to that as should have been expected, the Nigeria government, headed by Tafawa-Balewa as the first prime minister of the independent Nigeria; the northern and southern people did not accept either the idea or the demands being presented by Ojukwu and his contingent for a sovereign nation –Biafra- the killings and ethnic cleansing initiated by the northerners in revenge for the unceremonious and failed coup by younger officers inside the then Nigeria army and the unjust killing of most senior leaders in government which affected all the tribes making up Nigeria as a nation. The trouble erupted from the capital city Lagos, spreading down through the Midwestern states of Benin toward the Eastern region states composed of the ethnic Igbos. Odumegwu Ojukwu had the eastern region states of Nigeria under his control trying to rescue or secedes and pulls the Biafrans out of the Nigeria union because most people in the eastern region were not in agreement with the then system-setup.

During that war, there was total confusion and uncertainty; people were not sure what to do next and how. Many offices, as well as public and private institutions were packing up and leaving in haste for their respective hometowns. Those living near the targeted conflict areas were packing up and seeking temporary refuge wherever their instinct took them. Some of the villages like Ugbelle, far away from the areas of conflict, daily received distant neighbors who came in to take refuge in schools and churches and peoples' spare rooms and uncompleted buildings.

Military troops were being dispatched in trucks by the hundreds in convoys from the federal capital, Lagos, intending on recapturing the rebelling east-central region of Nigeria. The eastern region was meanwhile busy recruiting amateurs and guerilla fighters through the processes of persuasion, forced inscription and conscription, to help sustain their demand for a separate independent nation. Roadblocks and sentries were mounted everywhere. Spies, false and true heroes were springing up from every corner of the country. Children were taking delight and, advantages of the chaos and anarchy to play much more than was permitted in normal times--no schooling, no going to the farms and rivers to help their parents to fetch water and carry farm produce home after schools. All these activities were slowly diminishing because of fear of being conscripted into the army and taken to unknown destinations. Many youth were never heard of again, lost in unexplained circumstances like this. Many parents were afraid and usually hid their male children in the cellars in fear or suspicion of the captors; everyone was on their own, and people became unpredictable in a bid to survive. Because of fear of going to their farms and cultivating their farms, most families were unable to provide enough food for their teeming children. Many children out of hunger resorted to hunting and eating all sorts of rodents: Rabbits and Snakes became more appreciated as steak or cordon blue' lizards were hunted with vigor and eaten with pleasure, frogs became delicacies, insects; all categories became scarce commodities because of constant demands for them. I mean, we ate things during the civil war that, today, the idea alone could make you sick – strange beings, humans- we ate all sorts of leaves and tubers whether with pleasure or with displeasure, I can no longer remember, but I survived and I am alive to write about it today. Unfortunately, many children died from food poisoning, malnutrition than the bullets of the stupid-war. **Kwashiorkor!** Jeez have mercy on humanity! Forgive them their heartless stupidities and errors for they know not what they do, but, they believe they do know; shame on humanity for being so stupid and ungrateful on a large detonation.

KWASHIORKOR

Remembering that dreadful disease now as I write, my eyes are wet with tears, rolling and dropping on my writing table- watching a younger or older sibling gradually die while still alive – their eyes popping out of their skulls, their skin, swollen and desiccated, scaly like that of crocodiles' pus dripping underneath their dried skins which will then become a feasting place for hungry flies and other bastard insects alike! Then in a few days, their abdomen will begin to inflate like a balloon and grow bigger than that of a nine month-pregnant-woman- the child must usually die at that stage! Because of lack of adequate food in a rich world! Shame on humanity, shame on greed, shame on ignorance, shame on stupid pride; shame on you leaders, all of you for sitting, watching, and presiding over such inhumanity against humanity!

Everything was happening at the same time and so fast that most had no clue as to what to do or think about the lingering situation. There were sporadic bombings meant as warnings by the federal troops who were more militarily prepared because of external support and by others who were very confident they could run down the 'Easterners' in a day or so; as when there is a riot in a city and armed men and women sent to stop the riots by any means. The federal government was convinced of doing the same thing in the Eastern Area of Nigeria, but the bitter truth was that the civil unrest lasted nearly three whole years. There was famine, deaths in their thousands, disease and hunger that inflicted the worst malnutrition ever seen in centuries on the ignorant, poor, and simple, natural-living people. These were the people who had been at ease with their Petit-gods and daily rituals of thanksgivings to their unseen ancestors and the unseen God whom they could represent with the symbols of Sun, the moon, or even a regular tree. The Colonial people regarded them as 'superstitious' and 'idol-worshippers'.

Life was going smooth and easy for this nation until politics and hunger for power by most self- or public-proclaimed intelligent men and women began to use force to implement selfish laws for my beloved people and the entire Nigerian nation.

All the wars we are busy fighting today against each other begin always with such flimsy reasons behind which are such things as: greed, selfishness, aggrandizement and fear; those shall always remain the motivating factors for killing and torturing others with brutal hatred; as if those people being victimized, humiliated, and killed were the real problem of the world, as if killing and eliminating those ignorant and innocent people would better the situation of the others in the world. Humans are very peculiar in their ways of reasoning and acting. Humans are full of so many enigmas regarding their conducts or character traits; so many unanswered questions concerning humankind and their general concept of life continue to bother my mind.

The uncertainty continued for what seemed an eternity. The eastern region refused to give up their demand for an independent Biafra State. The federal government was not willing to concede to their demands. As time passed, the federal government began to lose patience with those agitating for independent nation and so decided to intensify their warning attacks and bombings. That new line of action heightened the level of discord between the Nigerian government and the agitating Easterners. Victims started to rise on a more serious note during this period than during the period of talks and negotiations that was on previously. It was not hard for the federal government to recapture Enugu State after some intense battles; they had the advantage of more people, better trained and equipped military men and in addition to foreign assistance. Consequently, the Ojukwu-soldiers (as they were called then) shifted their guerilla-headquarters to some unknown zones of the area--some said Abakiliki, some said at

Umuahia. At this stage, the war and its mutiny, maneuvers and strategy-laying, had consumed and lasted for nearly a year from the middle of 1967 into the middle of 1968.

A few schools and churches were still functioning with discretion. My school at Enugu was among the few schools still bothering to open their doors for whoever could come in and sit for learning. Most children spent the school days playing and chatting after school assembly and singing the national anthem - pledge to be humble and obedient to law and order-

One Wednesday afternoon at about 14:40 p.m. two jet fighters from the federal government troops appeared out of the blue and without warning started spraying bullets and grenades on the school building. They killed over fifteen children, including one teacher who happened to be my class teacher and damaged most of the school buildings and infrastructure. The majority of the children had already been on their way home when it happened otherwise, the victim numbers would have been much more elevated if the attack had taken place thirty minutes before the school closed. Thank God! Thank Chukwu Okike Abiama because I am still here today to talk about that crazy and nonsense war.

"Take cover! Take cover!" Everyone will prostrate instantly on the floor. That was the popular phrase and precautionary measures that the war volunteers taught the children, women and old people during that war period. That same day, the attacks were carried out in various places within Anambra State, inflicting abundant damages in one day alone that the whole nation would have to reckon with. A few hours after the attack, Lft. Colonel Chukwu Emeka Odumegwu Ojukwu declared a state of emergency, asking his followers to tighten their belts while they waited for the worst. "We shall resist to the last man among us, for the cause of our father and motherland". (The popular cliché used by all). This has been the first real state of emergency since the negotiations and upheaval started. Everyone became quite aware that the situation had gotten out of hand, and it was no more a child's play.

Soon there was a scene of mass exodus: women with children tied on their shoulders, all their valuables expertly balanced on their respective heads, and hands-free matching on ahead toward a non-predetermined destination. Most important offices were evacuated with their officers to some other secret and less vulnerable places such as Umuahia, Aba, or Orlu in Imo State. Many people decided to find their ways back to their respective villages in order to die among their kinsmen and women. Declan Obi, my uncle, was among the few privileged ones with a vehicle, for those it was easier to move and run. Two days after the attack, a state of emergency was declared by the officials in charge of this situation; in response to that call for action, my uncle, who was then the African Continental Bank manager posted to Enugu branch, took me, Edith, and Canice in his 404 Peugeot car with little or nothing and headed homeward; they joined the roads that were replete with desperate directionless souls searching to live and survive. Those who had no other places to run to stayed back with shaken fate, to stay and face their imminent destiny. The war gradually took a more serious dimension, extending and engulfing nearly the entire nation. All government and private activities were indefinitely shut down, including all the institutions of learning particularly in the East. Contrary to everyone's expectations and predictions that unnecessary war lasted for nearly three years because of mostly ethnic diversities as is common in many parts of the world.

Consequently, I, my uncle, and relatives were once more back together in our village, Ugbelle with nothing to do at such a time. No businesses, no schools, just gardening and subsistence living were all we could afford at the time. There was nothing of interest to attract the war all the way from Lagos or the Northern region to Ugbelle, my village. Most of the remote areas were safe; the war had no means to extend to such places that were sheltered with the help of abundant natural trees and thick vegetation. The people in Ugbelle depended on the radio information mostly flowing from the BBC and the VOA. Everybody was busy waiting to see what happened next.

By 1970, the Easterners who were demanding for the independent Biafra State after three years of struggling, toiling, and many lives lost, were unable to keep up with their resistance and the mounting pressures from the federal government who were being supported with arms and other essential ingredients by foreign governments--Great Britain, Russia and Germany in particular as I heard. (Because I do not know practically anything about that except the little I could now remember from experience and observation). Due mostly to many factors ranging from food shortage, ammunition and arms, lack of medical care and adequate health care personnel, there was simply shortage and lack of everything necessary for a realistic confrontation of war. The Igbos really did their very best: improvising ammunitions such as the Ojukwu bucket or Ogbunaiqwe, which was a locally manufactured bomb and very potent. "Ogbunaiqwe" means mass destruction. According to the most popular allegations, it is generally believed that the entire war was sponsored mostly by Lt. Connell Chukwu Emeka Odimegwu Ojukwu and few help from Gabon, Island, Israel etc.

The 'Ojukwu bucket or ogbunaigwe' was the main ammunition used by the Biafra for the war. There was only one rickety old jet plane as I heard growing up, and with local rifles and improvised ammunitions; the soldiers had no formal military training and no boots and military uniforms or real supplies. In such a condition and able to hold a war for so long, gained the Igbo peoples-- the Eastern populace of Nigeria--such international acclaim and recognition that many other countries began to pick up interest in the Nigeria affairs and that of the Biafra.

The Biafra could not go on though, so by January 15th 1970, they surrendered to the federal government under the leadership of General Yakubu Gowon. During reconciliation and peace processes, the slogan was "No Victor, No Vanquished." The civil war officially ended with this slogan. The peace and reconstruction of Nigeria was fast and easy especially, since they discovered abundant crude petroleum. Nigeria was immediately widely proclaimed as one of the richest countries in the world because of the high-quality crude oil discovered in many parts of the country, mostly the south and the south eastern areas of the country. Rich Nigeria!

15th of January 1970 precisely marked the end of a devastating civil war that had lingered for three consecutive years. Then followed the after war effects and activities. People began to gradually retrace their ways back to what used to be their residence that had been damaged in one way or the other during the civil war. The federal government and state governments joined hands to facilitate a quicker rehabilitation, restructuring, and restoration program. By September of the same year, the children were back to school; life was returning to normal everywhere.

I and my siblings were growing in age as time passed by. I was barely eight, more experienced and growing into a strong and athletic young lad. Also now, a reasoning person, back again in Ugbelle with my biological parents and grandparents. Because of the war, everyone was forced to stay close to families and manage to live or die together. The school systems and standards were reshuffled and improved. There was mass unemployment, but soon there was too much for all to do.

Peace returned from nowhere to everywhere in the country; renewed energy with a high level of enthusiasm and optimism was felt among the citizenry. In the midst of that high energy running in the country's veins, Nigeria was declared by the international organizations in charge as having one of the best quality petroleum in their lands. They became the second largest exporter of petroleum and allied products in the world, after Saudi Arabia, and a few years later, a staunch member of the Organization of Petroleum Exporting Countries (OPEC). Consequently, people began to get rich and richer in material wealth, the opportunist scampering and hustling for the big money. Nigeria became widely known as the "Rich Nigeria" within a space of twenty-four months. Foreign-made goods were pouring into the country with little or no control, as well as immigrants from all parts of Europe, America, Asia, and neighboring African countries in search of greener pastures.

The speed with which the whole thing started and progressed was indeed very alarming; so much so that in less than six months after the civil war, the negative effects and feelings of war were quickly forgotten, and the people's lifestyle and concept to and about life in general began to have notable and positive changes. There seemed to become a kind of positive mental revolution; the masses began to reason, think, and talk about the affairs of the world beyond, not only about Nigeria like in the past. Enlightenment oozed from every corner and everybody. As Adam Smith said in his book of economics and over population, control measures "that war also serves as a measure of population control and a resultant betterment of life for those who survived the war tragedies." The surviving Nigeria/Biafra began to live well. Designer's products continue to find their ways into Nigeria, mostly from Europe and America. Mega grocery shops and multi-national businesses like Kings Way stores, UTC, Marks & Spencer, Levi, you name it and they were all in Nigeria. Julius Berger and many others for construction and virtually everything were coming into Nigeria. Concrete houses, schools, and hospitals were busy springing up in all corners of Nigeria. There was what they called an "Oil Boom"!

Nigeria was in a different dimension or a 'born again'- unity and unification talks, construction and reconstruction of virtually everything ranging from: roads, electricity, pipe-borne water, markets, schools and modern houses etc., even an attempt on a common indigenous language was made and to crown the post-war Nigeria with peace and quick recovery from the war aftermath - the oil boom of the same seventies which propelled our nation into the global petroleum exporting countries (OPEC). This meant wealth for Nigeria; member of the richest countries of the world! The money started flowing in till today from Crude Petroleum.

As the money flows into our system, so does corruption, loss of Godliness and loss of patriotism. During the early seventies, as a child of barely Eight years of age, I remembered what my growth and that of my mates used to be- parties everywhere, everyday, even in the remotest villages' people find various ways to celebrate one thing or the other. There was a rich feeling of love and well-being thick in our atmosphere – you could breathe love, peace and security everywhere you go then, in all parts of my beloved Nigeria: North, South, East and West; and even beyond! In those days, we used to play from morning until the following day without sleep, straight to school and back, continued playing, joking, laughing and eating without tiring. Even in today's devastated Lagos, we used to put our tents and sleep out of the houses, almost all neighborhoods were enjoying that fresh evening breeze under the imperious moon shine so bright then to read even poor calligraphic writings made on sand floors; clear blue sky outpouring those tantalizing and twinkling shinning stars. How can I forget the impact of pain and the sweet sensations of yesteryears in my great nation?!

Today, as I sit writing, I bleed and hope for a better Nigeria; a better Nigeria with the same sweet sensations of the seventies without which, I will no longer retain my honest praise and respect for Nigeria as a sovereign nation, if we can bring this entity – Nigeria to the same state and with same peaceful constitution from the seventies, I will frankly suggest a referendum for restoration of a real federated nation where each constituent regions can manage their ethnic people and natural resources within their own pace. My unshakeable hope is highest for even a better Nigeria, the sky is our limit! God is with us, though, the devil is fighting harder to disintegrate us and bring sadness to our joyous minds. Trust in God! We will prevail above all obstacles and still come out in flying colors. It is written everywhere; it is in the wind that we shall soon become a greater nation than ever before! Do not despair, my brethren. God is on your sides!

UNIFORM LANGUAGE FOR ALL NIGERIANS

What is language?

A dictionary defines language as: "the particular form of sounds or words used by a nation or group". Based on the above definition and in my desire to find a peace-laden-solution to these long-lingering challenges engulfing the entire amalgamated nation - Nigeria-

Obviously, Nigeria as one nation has got no known language which represents and unites us as one people from the same ancestors and that maybe the main reason why Nigerians are people with talents yet, unable to unite and launch solidly into the technological world and make things happen. That may also be the reason why we lack that sense of patriotism necessary to ginger-up enthusiasm and motivation for people to work and die for their country. Maybe lack of a uniform language is the cause of the reason my fellow Nigerians have no respect for any form of laws and orders in the Nigerian context as a nation while the same Nigerians individually are very law abiding people by nature etc.

HAUSA, IGBO, YORUBA and other minor ethnic languages spoken in Nigeria are not accepted as the national language of Nigeria as a country. Our collective indigenous languages as a people before Nigeria was created by foreigners, have been battered, trampled upon and are referred to as dialects or vernaculars. The said languages represented for the people a form of expression and communication as indivisible part and parcel of a group descended from the same ancestors with ingrained cultural background; with inherited physical and psychological structures. These groups of people referred to as ethnic groups among other things did naturally inherit: culture, beliefs, language, technology etc. which is what is lacking in the Nigerian hierarchy as a nation. Nigeria as a non indigenous nation did not inherit any of the above legacies as being inherited by a people from the same genealogy.

 We all know the history of Nigeria; how different ethnic groups of people were deceived and forced together by the colonial Pirates to form a nation of their choice and their language duly imposed on them.

The above narrative represents Nigeria for all of us and the main reason why at 56-years of self governance, Nigerians seem not to have a sense of direction, no definite goals and aspiration; none of the various ethnic groups feels he or she is a bona fide Nigerian and we are all still struggling with language and communication problems. From observation and analysis, lack of common language is one of the fundamental barriers obstructing and hindering the smooth progress of Nigeria technologically, politically, culturally and otherwise. Does the above premise in anyway define the past and present Nigeria history or narrative? If so, what should then be the most viable solution and way forward to curtail most of the inherited challenges as a nation?

For any country to be sovereign should normally have a common inherited spoken language which all its citizens should be able to understand and speak fluently even without having attended the four walls of an academic institution; Period! Without that, the nation has no taproot; and a tree without taproots can hardly stand for long when the storm rages. A house without a solid foundation will soon sink and crumble under persistent rainstorms.

VIABLE SOLUTION FOR THE NIGERIA/ BIAFRA CHALLENGES

The only logical and valid way to bring any sort of solution or remedy to a problem or situation should be to firstly, identify the main issue or situation at hand causing the problem, and then, analyze and decide on a more viable approach which will definitely bring a lasting solution to the given problem. After having identified and analyzed the problem, work out a way then to contain them so as to yield and produce positive results for the benefit of those afflicted.

The Nigerian situation is unique; there are many issues, which require conscious solutions with determination and drive; the first in the list of factors hampering real progress and prosperity for both the nation and its citizens include:

Negative mental attitude

Language barriers

Lack of patriotism

Superstition

Negative cult and fraternity

Hero and Idol worshiping

Ethnic differences in tradition

Culture and mental concept

Corruption and embezzlement

And above all is- Religion

Those are among others, some of the the main disturbing factors negatively affecting our beloved Nigeria and the region of Biafra as a race. And to contain and curb these lingering issues and to put them into perspective and to lead Nigeria and other regions back on track, we must start a basic national building with a set out aims and aspirations to duly restructure our academic system and education method for our children. Below are the first and necessary procedures:

●●☐   Create a **NIPH-** *National Institute for Peace and Harmony-*

Solution- in accord with Natures' laws there is no way anything tangible and durable for peoples' benefit can be achieved without the inner commitment of faith and determination to achieve the desired thing or object. My deep concern for the present and potential problems lurking at every corner in my beloved Nigeria/ Biafra had given me this pretty idea to setup a kind of institution where the business of life and living will mostly be taught to growing children; A school where the importance of living life with positive mental attitude at all times will be mostly imparted on growing children and above all, an institution where the Golden Rules of Nature´ or Creation will be their prime subject and ultimate goal.

To achieve this will consist mainly in the gradual re-education of children and people of Nigeria through practical education hinged on examples; retrieve as many children as possible from the present negative mental trend back to the positive mental attitude. This project will need between fifteen to twenty intensive years (15-20 years) of coaching before result can be seen and will then continue to propagate and populate with generations of positive minded Hausas, Biafrans or Yorubas who shall be full of love and patriotism for their respective nations and people.

How Shall the NIPH Begin and Function?

●● Firstly, we should search and select five boys and five girls (5boys-5girls) from each of the thirty-six (36) States of the country apply and inculcate in them the NIPH ideology. Approximately 360 students will begin the program. Their ages will be between 4-6 years old children living and training in the school till they are approximately 20years of age. On graduation, the 180 boys and 180 girls will on a national consensus be allowed to take over all forms of leadership positions in Nigeria and bring to light all the positive principles of life they were taught at school into their leadership aspirations. It is as simple as that, the trick is in the training; the gradual impartation of positive wisdom.

The infallible cosmic laws of creation when properly applied in any venture concerning life of humans and animals cannot fail to yield effective deliverance which will surely as the sun rises every day, lead us all to peace with love and harmony for generations yet unborn.

This will be the first positive step in a bid to rebuild our beloved Nigeria and reeducate my awesome people on the right side of things of creation. Just a try of this principle is my pledge; all I ask for this book! While the school is going on, we will hold national forums to discuss the next vital issue on the list, which shall preferentially be:

●● LANGUAGE: All Nigerians should be made to speak one common language; local or foreign language is unimportant so long as the chosen language could be widely spoken and written by every Nigerian in and out of schools. (By adopting any of the existing languages or device an entirely new language).

●● RELIGION: Adopt just one uniform religion for entire nation or abolish any form of public worshiping. (people can pray and worship their God better in privacy as we do with our personal affairs)

●● Device a common cultural exhibition which will be able to represent the entire Nigerian image and not as tribal cultural shows depicted as the general Nigerian culture. If we have no common culture as a nation, we can device and develop one for ourselves.

●● Spirit of patriotism should be allowed to foster through leadership by example. I.E., doing the things we preach as politicians or as leaders.

●● Abolish any form of negative cult that preaches violence and causes harm both to members and others.

●● Reform our armed forces starting from the Army down to the Customs with the right work ethic and sound patriotism as their 'watch-word'

●● Bring back all Nigerian citizens in prisons all over the world and reintegrate them back into the main stream of the society and create equal avenues and work opportunities or incentives for them to design and create their own work for livelihood

●● Setup a big association for 'Talented Nigerians' whose job among others will be to boost Nigeria interest and industrialize the entire nation through unconditional humanitarian initiatives etcetera.

Nigerians as individuals are very brilliant. God gave us everything in excess. They are people with the ability to learn and adapt faster than anyone else in the world. Therefore, nothing can stop us from making it to the zenith of human possibilities!

Ladies and gentlemen! It is now time for real things to start happening in our country! Let us get down to business, we have played too fu**ing much! Now is time for spiritual and national awakening; if the size and the nation's diversity is withholding or slowing a fast national progress, freedom of expression and patriotic actions, then, therefore, divide the nation into two or three ethic national groups as existed before in the past, so we can have the chance to observe the differences in progress and wellbeing in the course of time; alternatively and more simply and cost effective and viable should be to hold an honest referendum and agree on the best way forward for all…Nigeria as a sovereign nation is long dead and rotten as an entity since after the discovery and refining of petroleum in the South-Eastern regions of the amalgamated country!

RESTRUCTURING AND RECONSTRUCTION OF NIGERIA/BIAFRA

For African nations to move positively forward, Nigeria as a huge nation amongst them must stand firm and strong on her feet to achieve a positive progress. To do that, Nigeria should kick-off by restructuring her cities, living styles and improving the social conditions of her teeming and ever growing population.

Your question should be how do we begin and succeed permanently with these tasks?

We should henceforth acquire through persuasion and amicable agreement, all the barren or fallow lands in the entire country, out of a sincere and organized national planning structure and do the following:

-Device or implement a uniform plan for further usage and or development of acquired or appropriated lands in such a way that must definitely benefit the entire community who live within that vicinity; where the land appropriated originally belonged to them- depending on the plan of action adopted by the government to achieve that.

-On the land belonging to a particular community, duplexes will be built in a uniform order; it will be simple but, with all the comforts of modern houses.

-These houses should always be built in the middle or centre of any of the lands to be constructed, and must have sizable balconies or terraces front and back of the building to allow residents to make adequate uses of the extending lands back and front of the constructed houses.

- The houses built or around the centre of the given land, and each sides of the land uniformly divided should be used for recreation and parks for that community to entertain; and, for farming with the aim to guide the communities to be-self-sufficient through farming and agricultural productions, right on their community lands where they live.

-The amusement park should endeavor to include all possible recreation and amusement facilities imaginable for the entire community in the new Nigeria housing projects, soccer pitch, open and closed gym spaces and equipments, tennis, basketball, swimming pools, cultural arenas etcetera should include in any further construction plans in any part of Nigeria or Biafraland.

-The both sides of the constructed houses should be adorned with a vast farmland that must be divided chronologically, equally and uniformly for every family residing in that community and owns any of the constructed houses.

-From the constructed houses to the end of the farming land, there will be a uniform warehouse or store for the residents. The warehouse will ensure space and easy storage of their farm products which, can be transformed, reserved or sold directly from their stores to the public.

The idea of this is to encourage people to live in their houses, farm within their houses with their families and transact their daily businesses within their communities. Their excesses will be sold direct from their farms to the public from the public warehouse...access to main roads must be provided to those communities for easy transportation of their farm products to sell for money when they have the social need for money.

-Structural and Architectural Designing of Acquired Lands- *A new outlook forNigeria/ Biafra*

-Road-warehouse or store-farmland (divided uniformly according to land size)-house in duplex in a row (sized according to the land acquired)-vast park-road-refuse storage and recyclable-void. (I will present the feasible structural design on a separate format for that laudable plan when the community or governments are ready to accept or further my ideas).

The Nigerian government should henceforth endeavor to confront many of the basic issues presenting enormous challenges to our beloved nation and her citizens; in the areas of: waste disposal, electricity supply, clean and running water, central drainage system, and good roads to our mansions etc.

We should invest a good amount of our oil money into a central drainage system. For electricity supply we should go -Solar- Solar energy should be used fully to generate our electricity; let all our oil money be flushed into that sector alone if the need be! Same for water supply! We shall gradually reconstruct our old cities with the same shape and infrastructure, gradually and systematically rebuilding them. Let us better worry about that with the passage of time when we are ready to implement a lasting solution to most of our current and past national quagmire.

POLITICAL RESHUFFLE ANCHORED ON UNITY AND PEACE FOR NIGERIA/BIAFRA

The first true manifestation of this project will start to take effect immediately after the selected students of NIPH – *National Institute for Peace and Harmony*- have graduated or finished their unique coaching. Like in my book "Global Code for Peace and Harmony", the students shall begin their leadership assignment by firstly drafting a New National Constitution that will attune and harmonize that change due to be made in order to enable them drive an easy and smooth mandate. The students will be made to apply the same simple and practical philosophy as contained in my book – Global Code for Peace and Harmony-.

Below is an excerpt from my book "Global Code for Peace and Harmony". My reason to include some of the pages from that book in here is to make it possible and easier to implement the humanitarian principles of fair and just leadership on State and national levels. If for any cogent reason we are not able to implement these principles at a global perspective. In that case, all nations can implement the same leadership principles in every respective system of government; consolidated and anchored on the given and proven principles that lead to peace, unity and harmony!

I have said earlier that the Nigerian economic, social and political problems are not unique. No nation in the world today has a unique problem. Our respective national problems have their foundations on the Elite-Political-System-Design; of which, money and power are the ultimate goals.

To gain peace, unity and harmony, Nigeria as for other nations should do well redesigning their political structure to embrace more of humanitarian countenances; doing that will surely breed trust and confidence among the citizens and also ensue a deeply rooted patriotism that will give people reason to serve with enthusiasm, love and determination, instead of sabotage, cheat and betray each other.

Below are the steps to follow:

PART 6

BLUEPRINT FOR EFFECTIVE LEADERSHIP

– New National Constitution Based on Majority Voice-

Having been to places, seen, tasted and contemplated; often, deep down within, I have also been humiliated; I have enjoyed, cried, laughed and reacted to all the human essences of life or living.

I have equally questioned the Creator, the devil, the leaders, the parents, the teeming people and friends along my life's journey; but, unfortunately, I am yet to receive cogent answers to those mountains of questions and actions culminating to the looming and pervading global challenges. I could not stop but to worry about my beloved world so much so that, I am tired; neither could I stop being angry for the ways humans around the world seem to mislead one another. In my obvious frustration and worries, I received this 'Divine Inspiration' to join in 'This Inevitable Race for National/Global Reshuffle and Reconstruction'; this is the renaissance…

As I chose to dedicate my entire life to knowing and studying humans around our globe in addition to their respective ways of life, to my dismay and chagrin, I discovered that about ninety percent of what we term 'National or Global Problems' are duly caused by humans themselves and not by the actual creation itself!

Other questions came about as a result of this shocking discovery:

What are the reasons why humans cause problems; create confusions and frustrating circumstances for themselves? Is it out of ignorance or out of malice? This topic should be open for global debate; but, for me, I will suffice to assume that they acted and continue to act out of **-Ignorance-**, which means: having little or no knowledge of things, situations or circumstances, in the right way they should be and function.

Why do I choose to believe that humanity is acting out of ignorance?

Because to act with malice, is a remote sign of ignorance. To act out of malice or any other way other than, the ways that are universally acceptable for peaceful and harmonious coexistence is tantamount to the unawareness of the penalty; which, is shared on an equal ratio to the level of thought or action taken.

These factors are some of the subtle laws or sequences of nature. Not doing things right means that one is ignorant of the best practices or that one is intentionally acting with the wish or desire to do wrong or harm to others or to things.

I wonder therefore, what kind of human spirit could act with such inhuman malice? Unless, the story of the "Devil or Satan deriving pleasure out of peoples' distresses" is true; nevertheless, even if it's true that the devil likes to see innocent people suffer, I will choose to say that, the majority of humans are truly ignorant of what life and living is all about. Based on this premise, I had come up with the only durable and viable solution to help resolve most of the human and environmental problems on national and global perspectives.

All human life is coordinated deep down within their respective minds. Therefore, by balancing the equations of our respective minds, we can then balance the rhythms or equations of our respective lives; so doing, we can be able to achieve Peace, love and Harmony on regional, national and global perspectives.

The following are my lines of thought and action, which without doubt, if duly respected and applied by all global citizens, will make it possible to achieve that collective global objective which is – to make this world a better place for all and sundry. The only way is to initiate a program for a total re-education of the masses; teaching them the truth about life, as we know it with honesty and sincerity and guiding them to the right pathway to – unity, peace and harmony through positive deeds. Knockout all acts of treachery, deceit and wickedness if we must again in this world ever feel the essence of love, unity and peace with each and every human being, plants and animals! Obviously, achieving a universally accepted leadership structure and practice, the following consideration and steps must be paramount in the making:-

National Institute for Peace and Harmony- NIPH

Down the line of human history from time immemorial, there has never been any era marked with peace, love and harmony. In its place have always been brutal wars, massacres, supremacy, tribalism, and intimidation and discrimination etcetera.

Why not the other way around to foster love, peace and harmony instead of wars and chaos?

Is this supposed to be the true nature of humankind? Or did something go wrong during creation? These issues of wars, killing of one another, betrayals, cheating, and discrimination of fellow man and woman never seize to challenge my scope of imagination.

I do not want to go into details of all the personal troubles I was subjected to from childhood, seeing these negative human conducts against one another; especially, intuiting and with the deepest feeling that, we could do much better than that. As a result of that deepest feeling to see and live in a world where: love, peace, unity and harmony reigns supreme, I became irresistibly inspired to coin together and portray for perusal this piece of proposal as the only viable avenue for national or global peace, unity and harmony.

Certainly, you will wonder what gave me the authority and boldness to delve into this 'Sacred Topic'. You will find your answer in my first and endless book **-Universal Child-** I truly have paid my dues to the Creator, to Satan and to the human-made-system all to my own peril. And based on all the challenges, my blind adventures and fights to remain afloat in this daunting ocean of life today as I sit writing, I strongly belief that, I know enough about myself. In addition, I also know enough about peoples' mind-set; which is making it possible for me to write this piece of proposal for national unity, peace and harmony that had been meticulously structured to succeed against all odds.

-NIPH- National Institute for Peace and Harmony

For any viable and proactive change to take place in this region, in this world as of today, a global change of mental attitude towards all created entity will have to be the first step ever. Humankind must learn to use or shown to apply what we term as: POSITIVE MENTAL ATTITUDE (PMA) in all their daily affairs; in relating with one another, in conducting any kind of business with each other; and in any effort to learn any tangible and valuable things of nature.

In anything whatsoever we desire to achieve in our everyday lives, a Positive Mental Attitude is all we need to do good deeds and to be rewarded with satisfactory feelings.

Without the full understanding of the potentials and benefits of 'Positive Mental Attitude' -PMA- in all our respective actions and reactions, the content in this book will not be of much worth; because the entire contents in this book are based on these principles-uses of-PMA-

NIPH is a didactic institution of learning structured to impart only Positive Mental Attitude to its students. The NIPH students will act as "the sacrificial Lambs". They shall be taught to shoulder the burden of learning, living and acting in harmony with the 'Golden Rules of Creation…

-PMA- shall be the major topic for the selected students; they shall structure and enact a practical and realistic New National Constitution after their graduation. After which, the students shall be awarded the unanimous mandate to rule the nation with love, peace and harmony. This is our only hope for Nigeria or any other nation to be duly united; any other process won't work.

The conduct and positive attitude of the students after their coaching shall serve to portray the authenticity of those everlasting and time proven Laws of the Universe, which, they have been appropriately coached and soundly taught during their fifteen years of study in –NIPH-

What is the Major Objectives of the NIPH?

The major aim of the NIPH will be to source, select and educate children who will be chosen from all the sovereign States of the country. The selected children will be taught to comprehend the meaning, importance and how to apply the basic Nature's rules in all human circumstances; and shall prove the infallibility of those time-proven laws of the universe at the end of their academic career, through cultivating good and positive deeds as they move along.

Open and positive mindset shall always make the best of everyone or nation who puts them into practice; and secondly, with their positive education put to test, the chosen children will then act as the beacon of hope for all citizens in all the nations. Obviously, no nation's problem is unique and there is no problem in Nigeria above repair either; with honest approach. The only problem is in our individual and collective Thought Direction and Frequency; when you think negatively, act negatively, your reward and ingathering automatically, will be NEGATIVE. On the contrary, when you think positive, act positive, your reward and benefit will automatically be, POSITIVE. This is one of the time-proven-divine-rules inherent from our birth. This certainty in mind, the NIPH students will be inculcated to follow this positive pathway which will reward them with the right mindset necessary for the best kind of national change, which will aim to benefit our national and global communities irrespective of race, creed or gender.

How do we Kick-Start this Level of National Project?

All we need to do here is, simply select ten brilliant children, between the ages of 5 and 6 years old, from every autonomous community in the Biafra. The children must be in the ratio of five boys to five girls from each community. The selection must be of uniform criterion and carried out only by unanimously appointed individuals; with an impeccable love for Biafra rooted deep down in their hearts. I will direct and see to the solid foundation and operation of the Institution.

In a similar way also, the school's staff and teachers shall be selected and groomed to the required level of understanding the Golden rules of the Creator'.

The media outlets as always have the total responsibility of making this good news reach every home and jungle around the four corners of this country starting up from the national leaders down to the rural Peasants; and to the domestic and jungle animals. Whomsoever that can hear, see and understand should be made to know that-the entire nation is voluntarily embarking on this very project of national change for the better; for peace, unity and harmony to reign supreme everywhere in order to replace the present system of terrorism, corruption, killing and sabotage without mayhem or confrontation!

To initiate this mega-project, we will best start up stage-by-stage:

STAGE - 1

Selection of children for the -NIPH-

NIPH will be made up of children between the tender ages of 4 to 6 years and will be selected from the four corners of our nation by a special group of people or staffs who, in turn will be chosen unanimously to carry out the selectivity exercises. Said group of people or staff will have to meet, sit and work out among themselves, a uniform plan for a smooth and impartial process at the time to select the ideal children for the institution.

All States must have to present a maximum of ten children (five boys and five girls) irrespective of creed, state, region or cultural background.

The type of people that will make up the group who will be responsible for selecting the required students must be of experts in the field of human psychology, authors of successful self help books, some acclaimed clergy men of God and last but not the least, some media "gurus". Those responsible for selection exercise shall look for children who are less prone to negative influences by referring to every child's family-background and immediate habitat at the time to make selection.

STAGE- 2

SELECTION OF STAFF FOR NIPH

As I said earlier, the communication media should play the most important role in information dissemination through: the web, television channels, radio stations and Newspapers etcetera.

This institution will be staffed by people with faith and belief that, yes, this project

Goal can easily be achieved. Through data and testimonials of their personal lifestyles given by neighbors is what the parameter for choosing them will be based on; they must be of positive attitude in most of their respective daily affairs.

It will be preferable for this institution to be mostly staffed by authors of self-help books, psychologists, and people who are already showing concern and giving their efforts to similar services with the aim of making this nation and world better.

To endorse or approve whom stays as staff and as a student shall duly be decided by the author of this book in collaboration with Foundation members yet to be endorsed.

STAGE – 3

LOCATION FOR NIPH

The stage three and final phase before the commencement of the project will be the location of the institution.

The national citizens shall unanimously have to decide on the most viable and effective location and modus operandi suitable for the realization of the school's aims and objectives. We will suffice here to give a brief idea of what-NIPH-Students should be able to do for our nation and world at large after their graduation; when they must have completed the program between the ages of- 15 to 20.

STAGE - 4

Students' Assignments after Education

-Promulgation of National Constitution and Leadership Mandate-

-NIPH- students will be assumed ready for their assignments at the age of twenty; at which age they must have spent about fifteen years of their lives in an intensive practical coaching. The kind of coaching imparted to the students will aim to inculcate the best moral codes possible for effective national governance.

The kinds of moral code streamlined within the **Rules of Nature;** and suitable also, for the achievement and realization of peace, unity and harmony for all national and global citizens; and with the other living and non-living species of creation; as well as to give a conscientious care for our national and global environment.

It will be expected that NIPH students must have mastered the advantage and importance of applying positive mental attitude in all affairs concerning humans and their ecosystem; the true and ideal meaning of **Leadership** (service by example). They will learn the reason to pursue a definite purpose in life, achieve and retain only success habit, and to seek why failure overwhelms people continuously and then fix the undesired issues.

Above all, the NIPH students must know and appreciate the advantages of applying a positive mental attitude and the disadvantage of also, applying a negative mental attitude in all their affairs.

They will know the importance of forming a '**mastermind alliance**' and the enormous value of harnessing the efforts of more people in pursuit of a definite goal.

When we are convinced beyond reasonable doubt for the good and the positive impact of the quality of education imparted to these selected children, that will be the moment to set them -students of the NIPH- free; to set them loose and out for the divine mission of positive national and change which they have worked hard to learn during their fifteen years in the NIPH premises!

STAGE - 5

Students Return to Lead Their Respective Community

Under specific arrangements, each student will now be allowed to go back to his or her respective State of origin after completing the program between the ages of: eighteen and twenty years under the impeccable and realistic training of -NIPH- and then, be allowed to lead their people to achieve divine unity, peace and harmony.

On their arrival to their respective States, all formalities will be carried out to officially receive them according to customs and traditions.

In my opinion, I should suggest that the said ex-students of NIPH should be received back home with open hands and seen as 'CHOSEN AND ANOINTED PEOPLE'.

Next step will be to immediately handover the leadership of every State and federal government to them with the unanimous support of the people and by the people.

Of the ten children who were chosen from each of the States (five boys and five girls), the first choice to head or lead any of the States will have to be the female genders; and then, assisted by their male colleagues. The rest of the graduates should be assigned to head other branches of the government that are considered delicate or prone to massive corruption.

On an appointed date, all the prospective new or 'experimental' leaders shall be sworn into office; and with that, the hallmark of a new era in the history of our country!

STAGE - 6

Commencement of Duties by the Ex-NIPH Students

To commence duties officially by those special students, series of meetings and national conventions should be held by the parliament or by a chosen group of statesmen that will discuss and bring into perspective all urgent matters upsetting the country and the world in general. In addition, to review the ways or modus operandi with which each student/leader will have to execute his or her leadership assignments.

There are many fundamental issues to be addressed and tackled with the main aim to trigger the wheels of peace, unity and harmony all around the country.

From my personal conceptual analysis of creation in general, the conscious and unconscious experiments carried out incognito, I can so far pinpoint some of the major causes for national and global unrest from time immemorial to this present day.

In my view and to the best of my knowledge, I have compiled a list, in order of importance, most of the issues that need reviewing and correcting with urgency for this nation to move farther forward and to function smoothly on a positive perspective.

The issues listed below are paramount in my list of national and global challenges hindering peace and harmony in this country from the past to this present day. We will have to face these challenges with the help of this 'new and honest constitution' for the sustainability of all citizens and their respective environment! They will include reason, why, and how those new laws could foster national and global unity, peace and harmony if and when effectively and appropriately implemented in our national and global political systems.

Amongst all, the first issue which will foster national peace and harmony in my scale of preference is – **Language-**

COMMON LANGUAGE

-Common Language for every Sovereign Nation-

A dictionary defines language as "The particular form of sound or words used by a nation or group"

Taking the above definition into perspective, and applying the natural rules of things of creation, in all essence; it becomes imperative that a **common language** for all nations be carved-out to compliment this new order of things. A uniform language for every national-citizen will help to form the nucleus, the engine and wheel of unity and oneness among citizens which we all desire.

The Creator Himself did a very good job in classification of the living and non-living matters into species. Each specie flock together in response to the natural law of similitude: 'like species flocking together', as it is for fishes, ants, and birds' etcetera. So also, should it therefore be for humankind as common and unique specie amongst others.

Therefore, it will be to the best interest of this nation to devise a common language for all citizens so as to help bind them more closely together. In Nigeria, for instance, majority of the citizens who never had the opportunity or a good reason to attend schools cannot speak English language. Such group of the citizens cannot read, write or speak English language and are therefore, automatically forced to live out their respective or collective lives in the margin of the society; irrespective of their natural potentials. This is a major drain for our nation and those of other nations in Africa and also to other continents of the world.

When people from the same country speak the same language, that sense of togetherness, brotherhood and neighborhood cannot fail to maximize the collective national energy force that will usually help to boost unity, peace, progress and harmony, if all things remain equal.

Do you ever feel embarrassed when you are unable to communicate with your fellow human from the other region of the country or continent?

Do you enjoy that feeling of frustration when you cannot express yourself in front of someone if and when you are out of your region of the country? I doubt any sane person will relish in such embarrassments.

Good news is that, such circumstances can easily be rectified just by **making all national citizens to speak the same language!**

To be realistic, irrespective of the language challenges in the entire Nigeria, as one people, entire humankind is supposed to use one particular form of sound or words to really make them feel like one in a family; to make them understand one another anywhere anytime.

It is obvious that the use of a common language is the principal factor that identifies and unifies people as a race or a tribe.

This fact in mind, I feel and believe without an iota of doubt that, if all humans, as one and unique specie could speak the same language, neighborhood and brotherhood will surely foster; plain understanding and acceptance of one another surely must foster; tribalism, discrimination and racial sentiments will gradually fade away and die a natural death.

The aim of this mission is to seek for a durable change in our national and global mindset while dealing with each other anywhere anytime. To teach all citizens of our great nations and the world at large to think and act positive; doing so, shall help to make most people better humans. In addition, such sense of oneness will definitely transform our respective nations and the world at large into a better place in where we can live and enjoy the beauty of this world and overriding the hard-core challenges that loom ahead. At least, we can confront the surging challenges with love and a positive mindset since those natural challenges will ever remain inevitable just for being part and parcel of natural creation.

"Enough of the old system of doing things in this nation"! This old system of things has continued from the beginning to hinder, hamper and jeopardize all national possibilities for peace, love, unity and sense of brother/sisterhood. Time is overdue to fix all these situations negatively pervading the minds of all citizens and their environment.

In perspective to the complex national problems, **common language for all national citizens** among other things should be the first fundamental assignment for the ex-students from *'National Institute for Peace and Harmony' NIPH to engage in.*

How Do We Convene National Representatives?

We must all sit around a table with food and drink to discuss how to carve-out or create a language every national citizen will speak, write and understand. From the look of things, we need to find a possible and easy way for all the people of this country to learn to make the **'same sounds and speak the same words'**. When we can achieve and put this into practice, the reward shall be a positive sense of oneness that nothing else can offer for now; also promote peace, unity and harmony to such extent never seen in the history of this pretty country!

A race is carved out of the language they speak; and the language a race speaks makes them an indigenous race.

Secondly, in my list of factors negatively affecting national peace and harmony is **'Money'**- money stands strong as the second most urgent factor to confront and correct for this nation and the world to move forward!

The question will be- how and what do we do about money and the use of it?

MONEY

-Use of One-Currency for all Nations-

From the look of things, money has gradually found its way into the mainstream of the entire   human-race and hijacked their natural sense of sound-reasoning; making them think and judge   only of and in monetary values. People are busy acting for money, working for money and ultimately living out all their precious lives for money!

Today, in the more modern era of the long history of humanity, as I write, money stand as next to life on its own for our assumed modern people.

These days, nearly every human being thinks and believes that he or she has to make and save money, in order to be able to live a 'real life'. Recently, this has become a global assumption; and without doubt, this very negative notion is instigating most people to perpetrate majority of the anti-social and heinous conducts currently pervading and overwhelming the present generation of human race.

As language, money stands firm as the second most important weapon that can be used with wisdom to enhance en-masse, the unity of humankind as people in love and at peace with one another. On the contrary, the same money possesses the power to disintegrate and tear humanity apart as enemies irrespective of living and dining under the same roof.

The worst and most improper way to expend one´s precious life here on planet earth is to "work just for money"; the most proper or holistic way should be to work directly for your food from nature between you and your family; the surplus sold, exchanged for other needed foodstuffs, or shared among friends, neighbors and relations. That should be the most humane approach to money and material accumulation; that is the proper way humans were created to work for living…In this new era, we should strive to beautify our people in every nation instead of beautifying parks, allotting acres of land to play golf, diverse constructions etc. In the place of all that, we should start by making enough land available for every community for them to share or use freely amongst them in order to cultivate their daily food within their respective neighborhoods, instead of working for just money in order to buy food later; what sense does that actually make?...

What should the benefits be when all nations use one common currency?

Use of common currency for all nations will benefit us in the following way:

- Help to unify humanity as one family irrespective of the fact that we live in different and diverse geographical locations.

- It will help to globalize most human aims and objectives, letting people have similar dreams and goals that will favor their national and global interests.

- It will encourage world citizens to desire with honesty to work together with enthusiasm toward the same goal and also, making use of standard parameters to conceive, believe and achieve their set goals.

- It will surely limit or mitigate most of the current and surging immigration and emigration challenges.

-Use of common currency for all will help to encourage majority of the youth to stay back and improve their respective 'corner' of the world with their natural potentials. Instead of abandoning their lands to wither, while they go hunting for bigger, quicker and easier ways to make money wherever they think it will be possible. What about that sense of illusion upon disillusion which happens to be the real feelings that will constantly dawn on you as you move ahead in your respective vain pursuit for money, under the man-made-rules?. Surely, at the end of your days all your money pursuits will always turn out as **'just vain pursuits'**.

Money, they say "is the root of all evil"- do you agree with that cliché? Money is not evil itself; the appropriate use of it either. It is rather, the bedrock upon which lots of good and bad intentions and actions are made manifest.

The major problem in this context is 'not about having money or not having it'; the major problem is that the perpetrators or inventors of the use of money had bad intentions; they never made it so that people can have it with ease and on uniform criteria. It had always been a case of the 'winner taking it all' irrespective of what happens to the rest of the citizens, whether they live or die never bothered no one in particular.

In fact, for most 'Bosses' and 'Leaders' it was preferable if a majority of the people suffer and die for the few to have more money and material possessions. The world has continued to surge along based on that erroneous premise since time immemorial.

Too complicated for me to imagine and digest how sane people could invent things that create so much stress to obtain and own as it is today regarding to 'money'.

I want to assure you that, you can always live comfortably well enough anywhere, anytime with or without money; if you only know how to implement the 'Golden-Rules of Life' in all your daily affairs. Money is not created, but invented; therefore, can never be more valuable than anything created by the Creator to deserve all that attention and sacrifices dedicated to its search and acquirement.

Now, having seen a few of the numerous advantages of using a *common currency for all nations;* let us briefly look at the various –

Disadvantages of not using a Common Currency for all Nations:

Money they say 'is the root of all evil'. Why that age long belief or axiom? Simply because every bad or anti-social activity taking place in the entire world from the past to the present day had always been for 'monetary purpose' or desire to make money; and possess more fame as well as material things, and ultimate power. This is the greatest illusion of all times; the greatest myth in the human history after Religion!

Money therefore happens to be the major factor causing most of the simple and heinous crimes in all parts of the world today, such as armed robbery with intimidation, hijacking, kidnapping, human and drug trafficking, prostitution and pornography, betrayals etcetera. The majority of the national and global problems today have links directly or indirectly to money; so are the national and global wars and political unrests.

Frankly speaking, it goes far beyond my human comprehension to understand why nothing has been done in all these years to permanently tackle this "powerful ghost" – Money-

Money had existed among us for centuries and its effect is always on the negative pathway. Money had always being causing man to enslave another in the guise of - creating work for him or her to earn 'money'. Humans have knowingly or unknowingly structured some kind of mental prison for themselves guised as money and wealth. We seek careers and be in bondage for our work which are chosen out of fear of not having 'money'; man licking the dirty shoes of another in order to make money; man plotting the death of an innocent fellow for the sake of making money;

man taking a woman in marriage and vice versa, not because of love and affection for each other but for money'. People going through all the humiliations connected with prostitution, trafficking and most deadly adventures all for money. The lists of the frustrating ventures and adventures which, most humans go through on daily basis for money are innumerable.

How do we Design or Create a Global '*COMMON-CURRENCY*'?

The easiest way to design a common currency will be to adopt one of the existing currencies or to design and print new currency as a global legal tender for all to use. The value of money is what it can buy, the satisfaction it can offer you, therefore, to accumulate wealth without deriving satisfaction out of it is worthless; the worst form of **vain-pursuit!**

There is nothing wrong with having money or becoming a multi-millionaire but, there is something wrong, when money is consciously used in such a way that may cause trouble for others; particularly also, when money is placed above people, creativity and wisdom. The national and global turbulences are not because of 'MONEY' but, because of human ignorance in major part; greed, fear of death and future uncertainties.

People should be made to know that they cannot eat more than their stomach can contain; else, it will explode. This is another way to ask people to stop accumulating money and material wealth they may never be able to use. How many people in history had ever said "I do not want more; I have got enough; I am okay and contented with what I have amassed? Why are many not using such phrases often? Fear for the future, fear of lack!

Let my people be taught to work enough to live and not to live to work- And to learn to lay more emphasis on creativity and selflessness than on money. Have respect and regards for other humans with or without-money.

In my view, I would rather opt for the old: **'BARTER-SYSTEM'**. The odds compared to the looming problems from the use of money as it is today will be more acceptable; or we could better unanimously adopt one of the most popular existing currencies such as **Dollar, Pound Sterling or Euro to serve as our global legal tender for all nations.** In addition, I feel that money and material possession should seize to be the yardstick with which to measure or determine the achievements of people and services to both themselves, national and global community at large. In its place- *'wisdom, degree or level of positive mental attitude (PMA) evidenced in a person's character trait (CCT), and amount or level of selfless service to others and environmental care will suffice'*. Such should become the basis for electing our true national and global icons henceforth!

The above are sequence of things we can do, and ways we can reason in order to foster stability, peace, unity and harmony for our respective nations and the world at large; as well as reduce crime, mass exodus, poverty and hungry and angry citizens in every nook and cranny!

RELIGION AND ITS PRACTICES

-One Religion for All Citizens-

What is Religion?

The dictionary defines religion as: 'any of various systems of belief or worship concerned with the spiritual and inner nature of man and usually, a super natural power recognized as creator or controller.

From the look of things, religion occupies the third position in the category of issues that largely affects and influences humankind. However, lately the good and positive religious influences on people and society have taken a downward turn; being diverted into very negative and mortal practices that is jarring everyone on the face and intruding in the form of belief chosen by others.

Truth is that the belief in something higher or extraordinary is a natural human characteristic; which best explains why we have these proliferations of religious organizations all across the world. In fact, there is hardly anyone who does not have something they belief in; be it: Mysticism, shamanism up to- Hinduism, Buddhism, Taoism, Confucianism, Shinto, Judaism, Christianity and Islam.

It is obvious from these proliferations of beliefs in something supernatural that, 'religion' as we have come to know it today and from the past, is a human invention to satisfy their natural cravings for guidance and protection in a life of uncertainty.

Our belief in a religion should naturally be a personal affair just like in meditation, thinking, urinating, sleeping etc. are all personal human affairs. Like all other living matters, all living things in the Ocean, Jungle, all the underground living creatures, humans are as well created without lack, humans are created to be independent with a fair supply of their basic needs as: food, water, shelter and clothing. Any other thing apart from those are nothing more than compliments and polishing of 'what there already was and still is'.

The good and bad Spirits silently living with you from the day you were born, should be the source of your belief; and the decisions and choices you make with them pertaining to the way you manage your daily and future affairs should rightly be your business with your innermost spirits and no one else's.

God and Satan live in you; they are your greatest teachers and your greatest ally, so what else are you searching for outside of yourself that you do not already have deep down within you?

The necessary natural principles and mode of conduct for peace and harmony for all humankind are boldly ingrained in the holy books; especially, 'the Bible' 'the Quran' and in all the ancient religions. They all embody most of the universally accepted moral standards meant for attaining a closer and more intimate relationship with the Creator to whom all human species tend to worship and glorify whether consciously or otherwise, and manifested through the demonstration of faith, hope and belief that the immediate future will always be better.

This is a way to encourage most people to be able to think positively and to do good while they await for their turn to toil, live and then die and be jettisoned to the promised land where they will hopefully find-love, peace and harmony as their final reward for all these worldly hassles of being Alive!

Creed, faith in a particular system of belief or worship, democratically speaking, is supposed to be a private and personal affair. Nevertheless, for whatever natural reason, religious worship is no longer a matter of choice but of force and sometimes intimidation. And each day, there are alarming surge of men and women of God; some are real while some are false. Too much interpretation and re-interpretation of the original laws set down from the beginning meant to lead to salvation and maximum fulfillment for all human beings. To add or remove any part of those divine laws tantamount to sacrilege against the unseen and silent God or Creator! (Because doing so, tampers with the things of creation, also obstructs the smooth process of the affairs of life for millions of world citizens)

For these reasons and many more, the ex-NIPH students will have to review the entire national or global system of belief and worship; and in like manner for: Currency, Language and other important factors obstructing nations and their God-given communities from achieving amongst them- peace, unity and harmony".

Nothing is absolutely impossible for humans to do if only they come together in unity with one idea pursuing it as a definite goal; surely, they will succeed to move forward towards realizing whatever their collective or respective dreams may be".

My View on Religion and Worship

How do you think the world would be if there be no more, any form of public religious worshipping; if global citizens were persuaded to worship their "Sacred God" in the comfort of their homes and if all the religions monuments on every global community be used as museums and sacred places for meditation?

-Do you think doing so will definitely remove or reduce religious fanatics, bickering and serve as a bridge to global love, peace and harmony?

Or

-Do you think we are too irrational to contemplate such proactive initiatives as possible gateways to find love, peace and harmony?

*To worship the unknown is strictly a part of the human intrinsic values. The desire and the need for humans to worship the unknown, to worship something, is part of the inbuilt psychic mechanisms, or psychic functions designed to stir up in us, the processes of **reasoning**. It is from reasoning that every other psychic function is activated: FAITH; HOPE; ADVENTURE; DISCOVERY and KNOWLEDGE... with these psychic functions stirring up within us; appreciation and the sensation of gratitude sets in deep within us in full force, and then, the need to express that energy force through worship will manifest – the birth of Religion!*

In essence, human need to worship is a psychic manifestation of gratification and appreciation. The inability to balance such psychic emotion or sensation stirring within us results in excess of religiousness; gradually develops into extremism and intolerance to other forms of expressing the same natural need to worship. Superstitions are another ways of expressing the same natural need and privilege to worship or appreciate life and the things life is made up of.

All that boils down to "FEELINGS and EMOTIONS" mere feelings and emotions in our own understanding, but in every standard, all the feelings and sensations are indispensable and integral nature of humans. Such action and reaction impulses make it hard, nearly impossible for any human to build or structure a long-term goal bound in love, peace and harmony without paying due attention to that insurmountable need and desire to worship the "Unknown" (God, Allah, Jah, Chukwu, Oluwa Harikrishna ...), Something or someone.

It is nearly impossible for humans to achieve any tangible life's goal without deep belief in the 'unknown' *something or someone.*

-In this context, in this premise, to worship is an embodiment of human nature; there is nothing artificial or superficial about worshipping whenever and whenever the urge surges from within you. The need and desire to worship form part of the numerous human phenomena and is best in private as in meditation.

-Religiousness is a good or socially acceptable attitude built or acquired along the trail of each one's life. Religion felt from the deep down within you, is not and can never be made a collective experience nor the expression of your religious feeling or instinct be done collectively – religion like sex, sleep are best practiced in private to be fully consummated.

-Everyone is born under varied geographical, cultural and parental influences. In this way also varies their respective experiences and manifestations of these psychic impulses in time to show gratitude and appreciation –through worshipping- for one's ability and immense struggle to sustain one's own life, and probably, that of others around or beyond; against most odds as diseases, hunger, pain and ultimate death.

-Fear is a psychic impulse as in desires, showing gratitude or hunger; whose function in all humans is irreplaceable. Fear serves to stir worship as worship stirs reasoning; both working from the opposite end of a psychic pole, every other functions and activities of our psyche rekindles in full flame.

Every global citizen has the unconscious need to worship the unknown. People should be on their own to or be persuaded to continue to worship, but should be practiced or expressed in the recess of their intimate privacy. People should hold sacred their respective belief in the unknown. Show gratitude everyday; appreciate all things around you. Commune direct with the unknown within you as in meditation; these are the best approaches to worshipping and the global religious bickering. We should encourage people to worship their Supreme within the recess of their habitat and keep their secrets with their Holy God. In their past, communities worshipped on their own and they live in peace and harmony with the general environment. Religious practices in this new era should be closely reviewed and modified.

The ball is right now on your courts. Let us do things from now for national love, peace and unity!

I wait for your sincere reactions to this fundamental topic. Do not take yourselves and your lives too seriously. Life is good; and the art of living is the most challenging of all arts. Become the prudent architect of your own life from now on; yes you can!

Simple Solution to All National and Global Religious Problems

The ex-NIPH students are very much aware that there is no defined or given system of worship for the Creator. That the true consciousness of God or the Creator is all embedded deep within every human. The students or "The Experimental- Leaders" will have to find a way to purify the religious sector from lots of false prophets.

In Nigeria as in other countries of the world there are increasing number of people of God who are mischievously proliferating those Holy Book and Sacred Premises. The NIPH students must seek ways out to make it impossible for false prophets, false men and women of God delivering any form of deceptive and unfounded messages to the vulnerable public, who are innocently seeking redemption and deliverance from the unknown.

I will suggest a uniform system of worship and belief for the entire human race. From the look of things, all the religious worship is focused on the same supreme being- one God or one Creator- Therefore, if so be it, why don't we all simply worship one God under the sam*e or different religious platform, for peace's sake?*

If all human races choose to worship the only CREATOR (if the CREATOR really needs to be worshipped) under one national or global religious platform; then we all will in turn benefit in the following ways: religious fanaticism will be on decrease; Riots and killings connected to religion will also decrease. Xenophobia and religious intolerance will decrease or cease out-rightly. Terrorism and suicide bombing will decrease if not totally end. Those minor problems are among the worst problems facing us since time immemorial; helping us in nothing other than, tearing nations and citizens apart from one another instead of bringing them close to one other.

DRUG, ALCOHOL AND CIGARETTE

-Legalize or Stop Their Entire Production and Distribution-

A lot has happened; so much is being said daily about drug, alcohol and cigarette. Obviously, the social issues concerning the above items seem to worsen progressively; instead of decreasing in proportion to the level of media publicities against them.

Turn on your TV or Radio set anytime of the day, there must be one or more incidents about these said vices. Most national and international publications- are talking about drugs, alcohol or dangers of cigarette every day.

People keep killing each other because of drug-issues; people caught and sent to prison because of drug; people constituting various social nuisances because of the effects of drug. On the other hand, people of various age hanging out in the city streets, some sleeping in bus and train stations for reasons connected to drugs or alcohol. Mortal road accidents caused by the negative effects of drugs and many more mishaps all directly or indirectly related to drug and alcohol.

On the other hand, are the Warnings and Alarm raised by expert doctors on the dangers and imminent death posed by the constant use of alcohol, cigarettes etc.

"WARNING: CIGARETTE SMOKING IS DANGEROUS TO YOUR HEALTH" yet, their manufacturers keep designing more attractive brands and propagandas aimed at selling more quantities and earning more money. So the proportion of youth that smoke is higher than those that don't and to worsen this social problem the very use of these prohibited or partially prohibited items seem to be taking dramatic increases in our social cadre. Here let us talk about just drug:

WHAT IS DRUG?

The dictionary defines drug as: "a substance used in the treatment and prevention of sickness or disease. It is also defined as: a clinical substance, especially a narcotic, taken for the effect it produces".

Over the past four decades or so, a lot has been happening in relation to narcotic: many families (as in time of wars or national disasters) have been broken apart; many have lost their dear lives caused by direct or indirect involvement with drugs and other intoxicant. Many people (especially the youths) have being continuously in and out of jails; while a good number of people as you read this, are still languishing in prisons for long periods of time for various laughable reasons; but, whatever the reasons it all leads back to drugs- its use, sale, manufacture and production.

GENERAL OVERVIEW

All of the above taken into consideration; it becomes relevant to add that this monstrous drugs form parts of the things of creation and therefore, they are as old as humankind and their history. Although, the main emphasis is on such metropolitan drugs such as: Cocaine, Ecstasy, Heroine LSD, Marijuana and Hashish etcetera.

However, the fact that those drugs existed and happen to be addictive by their selves should not have constituted any kind of problem for any one. Because, also, there are various types of poisonous substances growing out there which are also drugs yet, their benefits to humankind when properly used, are innumerable. The addictiveness of those drugs as Cocaine, Heroin are not the major problem but, rather, that aspect of human characteristics that when not disciplined, tend to push one towards over indulgence, which always leads to voluntary or involuntary abuse of things of pleasure.

This is to say that, there is nothing created by the Creator which is harmful; especially, if used and applied correctly. Even the food we accept and eat for sustenance, when wrongly eaten or abused, could also constitute an equal amount of disaster or ruin to an individual's comfort and well being. *Knowing the long history of humankind, nothing has ever been realized by human race without working them out by ourselves. Humankind had always had problems with their- emotions, the food they eat, the water they drink, the air they breathe, the children they have and etcetera.*

Your individual lives are in your hands; it's a fact of life. It is our respective duties as humans to manage our lives to a sound and high level of self- discipline. Things are meant to be born, live and die; everyone reasons, reacts and feels things. Is all that not a part of the freedom of expression and life as an entity?

All humans should listen and rely on their individual or collective efforts to control, moderate and discipline their needs and desires in conformity with the cosmic laws of the nature of things of creation. This is a compulsory natural duty for every world citizen. Our national and global problems and challenges are not just drugs, alcohol or cigarettes but, our wrong political values and dispensation of synthetic things or factors.

Therefore, the use of narcotic drugs, cigarettes and alcohol are easily controllable as hard as it may sound but, notwithstanding, it all boils down to- the mental attitude or the chemistry of mind-set of whoever that falls a victim.

Shakespeare visualized some of those human situations when he said: *"Our Problems are not in Our Stars but in ourselves"*. Meaning that, nothing is beyond our controls or management if we are sincerely willing to do so and keep it so real.

What should be the most practical and realistic solution to these drug related issues negatively constituting a menace in our nations and global communities?

In order to really put an end to the present drug issues and their recurring social hazards which are spreading like epidemic in all nook and cranny of the world today; there are basis to suggest that:

-Legalizing drug, alcohol and cigarettes should be encouraged.

-There is no way we can terminate the production and manufacture of drugs, it is one of the things of creation and fortunately or unfortunately, the remedy to most of our bodily ailments when appropriately used and applied. -Such drugs in context induce euphoria and encourage intimate personal and social relationships.

-The main advantage in legalizing drug use will be to minimize these needless break-ups of families by the unforeseeable problems inherent in the use, sale, trafficking and production of those narcotics.

-Legalizing those prohibited drugs will no doubt help to minimize the recurring currency laundering and may bring peace and new face-lift for many countries of the world marked 'RED' on global maps such countries as: Central America (Columbia), Afghanistan, Pakistan and many others.

-Legalization of those prohibited drugs will help to minimize the unnecessary and indiscriminate congestions of prisons, waste of work force from the part of unproductive people forced to live in jail for so long and the waste out of constructing and maintaining new prisons and their inmates.

-Above all, the legalization of those drugs will help to make them unattractive for those people who seek for quick avenues to get rich; or make a decent living without working.

-That will also help to bring back most of our talented youths who are being led astray through that monstrous and unproductive world of drug, delinquency and prison.

-If possible, let our reputable news media desist from giving constant and daily attention to those narcotic drugs- such approach is in no way positive. Because in compliance with natural human psychology; such an approach to the deep problem of drug can only help to attract more people going after drug because it is made too popular through unnecessary publicity; many go for it because it is trending; it is always on the news; this is a normal and common human characteristics. We all want to go with the latest on the news, with what is in vogue!

To achieve the above, the ex-NIPH Students- will have to devise an appropriate means and strategy to legalize the sale, use and dispensation of said drugs or narcotics creating only chaos.

LICENSE, SALE AND DISPENSATION OF DRUGS

After legalizing the use and possession of those drugs in context, the licensing and dispensation have to be worked out through national and global consensus. Every nation should be part of this and should be able to open their mind to this new way of doing things. Let us try this at least; and watch to see how this system will get better for all humans and entire ecosystem.

We should work out the modalities to manufacture and package the narcotics in well-controlled and safe doses; in similar ways to how other dangerous drugs are being prescribed by experts in the field.

All the polemic drugs or narcotics should be made to either be acquired endorsed and licensed outlets or obtained through medical prescriptions or be allowed in free market as with alcohol and cigarettes. They could also be dispensed in pharmacies or design a fresh and new establishment specifically in charge of all matters concerning narcotic drugs- its manufacture, dispatching, sale and usage. Money made from this venture should be properly managed.

-There is no doubt that this simple measure will surely help to sabotage the exorbitant drug prices which is pushing many youths into robbery and anti-social behaviors as evidenced everywhere today around the world communities.

-The simple logic here is- If narcotics ceases to be "quick-money-maker"- taking into consideration all human tendencies, desires and natural reactions to things and situations- those presently being dependent on its easy and tax-free income will naturally have to begin to search for other avenues to "get-rich- quick".

-This will also help to ease and relax the daily news features on drugs.

-Most families torn apart by drug related offences will then reunite with their respective families.

-Prisons will be decongested; lots of money and man-power saved and put into activities that are more lucrative to the public.

Above all, majority of our youths who are astray and in limbo due to drugs will be given due assistance.

This kind of move, if adopted by our national and global leaders will no doubt go a long way to ease most of the complications resulting from prohibition and orchestrated propaganda. We are all aware of the fact that nothing ever remains the same. Everything eventually must always make a change. Now is the time we should consciously begin to make certain drastic level of changes over certain rules and regulation which have been binding us now from time immemorial; we are hungry for change and freedom. We are hungry to do more things than we are allowed to do. In this new era of things, let us aim and focus on rules and regulations that will foster national and global peace, tolerance, unity and harmony. "YES WE CAN IF WE TRULY WANT"!

WEAPONS AND ARMED FORCES

Weapons are devices or instruments meticulously fabricated with the final aim to fight, defend, immobilize or instantly kill animals and even human beings. If the weapons are in metallic form, they possess the capacity to demolish houses and buildings. When composed of liquid explosives substances can demolish an entire ecosystem: plants, insects and animals of all categories.

The big question remains as thus: **That if weapons are meant to destroy and take away precious lives of fellow men and women, destroy houses and precious works of arts; plants and other living and non-living creatures, what is therefore the essence for their fabrication and proliferation?**

Yes, at a certain period in human history, out of ignorance or true necessity, people felt it was normal or even very necessary to have the best arm or weapon to defend oneself, family or place of origin. It was trendy and universally acceptable to fabricate and possess any kind of weapon one could design.

However, the human race has come a long way to this day with the ability to understand the good social need for unity, peace and harmony. The universe is now one big community through technological advancement; which is enhancing more integration, more unity with nearly everyone speaking the same language as brothers and sisters; in addition, wanting to be in harmony with the Creator.

With this line of thought, it becomes obvious that the present obsessive attitude of most people and nations to willingly fabricate and distribute weapons of mass destruction, is in no way the best move close to fulfilling that profound universal desire and quest for peace, unity and harmony at all levels!

But to restore discipline and orderliness in this 'war-torn-era and zones', the ex-NIPH will have to devise ways to harness all fabricated weapons of mass destruction from every nation in this world and set them up at a 'World Museum' for people from other planets to visit, take delight, and appreciate our human ingenuity and prowess in technological advancement. All the weapons can also, be assembled for the public to visit and see what their fellow humans have achieved in all these years.

If there is: peace, love and unity amongst humans, will there be any more need to fabricate and proliferate those destructive weapons?

The entire people and nations will soon be in unity with each other, in love and together as one people who are divided by zero; there will be no need for such weapons for fighting and destruction. There will be no more territories with borders to defend because our former frontiers will then become free for all humans to go in and to come out.

Do Humans Have the Natural Need for Weapons?

My answer is YES; we do!

-If we agree that the destiny of people is in their hands, so also their physical defense; should be in their hands as well. Putting this notion into perspective, it will therefore be advisable to legalize a short pistol with only two rounds of ammunition for every adult; and the present hunting guns still remain in use for the purposes of hunting and ceremonies in which gun shots may be required.

-Every man and woman has need for self-defense. Naturally, it is not wise for a human being to walk around unprotected with any form of instrument or weapon. Our world has always been a jungle where the fittest wants to live and feed on the weak.

Sometimes a family member may lose his or her mental equilibrium, and with the tendency to hurt people with a gun. For being the only one in that family who is in possession of a gun or any other weapon at that moment of mental derangement, how could we stop such a person from killing everyone around when found in such a situation?

Most of the times in situations like the above, before the arrival of relevant authorities to such a troubled scene- the damage is usually have taken place!

Sometimes also, it could happen that your pet-animals such as your dog or any other domestic animal may get wild and attacks its owner or any other member of the family or neighbor, what could you do to save the situation at such moment?

These things happen nearly on daily basis in different parts of the world at all times; and whenever they do happen, we should be able to contain them with ease; accept them as normal circumstances of life and contain such normal situations without undue panic.

Nevertheless, our duty should be to prepare and try to prevent major excesses. In view of the above line of reasoning, it therefore becomes very imprudent to out-law free ownership of defensive weapons for citizens who are supposed to be free and walking with their respective destinies in their hands.

Prohibition of anything whatsoever is a wrong approach to sustain peace and harmony. Prohibition obstructs the human nature for adventure. Unless there were other ulterior motives for the past and incumbent systems to place such outright bans on things as weapons, drug etc. otherwise, my pledge is for us to legalize every created thing and instead of outright prohibition, the best options for usage and application should be put in place as with many other things in our society; to coach and educate people on the best ways to handle and use the dangerous things!

-Assuming we accept the above suggestions; then the ex-NIPH students will have to set up a national or global body that will be responsible for the manufacture, licensing, control and distribution of any firearm released in the market through licensed and authorized dealers and manufacturers. There will still be wrong doers, but, we can always live with them and contain the wrong doers in peace and love as brothers and true sisters do.

-Initially, it will be pertinent to start this operation with 'gum-bullets' or others capable only to immobilize an enemy for two to three hours which will be enough time before help comes to one in a situation of attack or danger. You do not necessarily need to kill to bring or maintain peace.

-The hunter's gun can be maintained as it is or modified to suit the new system of things.

-Then, all the warships, warplanes, missiles and other weapons of mass destruction should be gathered and be assembled either in a chosen place or operated by a special body in each country that has possession of them. (This should be left to the discretion of the competent appointed body)

-Those weapons as monstrously dangerous as they maybe, in some degree, they portray and represent one of the highest levels of human ingenuity and technological advancement. Therefore, deserve to be treated with awe and admiration.

-Our Arms depot and most military barracks should be converted into areas for tourist attractions for earth citizens and for those visiting the earth from outer-space.

-Having done all that, the great men and women of wars (all the Armed Forces) should be set free and released from the camps and barracks; to go back to their respective homes, get some rest and have fun with families and then, begin to pursue their personal goals in life without brutal interruptions or interferences. If any of the armed force-men and women may wish to switch into other fields wherever their disciplined services may be required for the benefit of themselves and others; that can also be encouraged.

-Better still, majority of the armed force men and women should be organized to combine their united combat discipline into a united effort to battle and overcome food shortages, hunger and diseases through a unified global farming systems and disease eradication techniques.

-The high level of mental, physical training and discipline of a soldier, if conscientiously harnessed into any field of activity, will never fail to yield abundant fruits for all to eat and be merry!

-The soldiers have all it takes to set the engine of positive change rolling. I suggest we capitalize on the soldier's expertise to only save lives; and not take innocent lives away.

In a similar sequence, the ex-NIPH Students- shall have to meet and meticulously scrutinize most of the big organizations with many followers such as sports and religious organizations to find a way to make the most of their combined manpower or work-force to render more practical assistance to the governing body, in the field of **farming and eradication of hunger and diseases.**

Most men and women of God should team up with the military experts, devise a functional method to produce and provide food in abundance, and perhaps, shelter for the teeming populace.

- The road to the 'Promised Land' or 'Glory' is very far away; -hunger, fear, disease, lack of adequate rest and stress surely reduces people's chances of reaching their respective destinations and achieving their set-out goals.

-If humans could convert all or most of their energy and ingenuity that is being negatively invested into fighting and killing; arms manufacture and proliferation, humanity will surely begin to live in unity, harmony, healthier and happier environment.

- If humanity could invest most of their given potentials into positive ventures, such as farming, individual inventions, reconstruction instead of destruction, we shall do much better in all aspects. And if we could combine that with the abundant energy burnt by all men and women of God in worshipping, preaching and praying all day long; if these energy and talent are given into agricultural research and food production, no doubt the whole humanity shall have enough to eat and drink for a long time and want for nothing.

-People will be merrier and happier with their stomach full. They will be more enthusiastic about most of the things of creation; and the entire world will benefit most in a system replete with enthusiastic generation at work and as a people!

-The above suggestions may not bring a lasting solution to most of the present national and global problems, but, at least, we will be embarking on the best possible solution for the pervading challenges and imminent looming catastrophe.

-Doing things in the ways suggested above would show our willingness to seek for a lasting solution over these problems, which are challenging and overwhelming our national and global community. This is what counts most within man and God- doing our best and leaving the rest to the Creator.

In view of the above, I am confident that, if humanity could adopt the above initiatives – I promise, in a few years time, say ten years from then, every human will cease to worry about what to eat, drink and where to sleep or what to wear because we have enormous potentials capable of turning anything whatsoever around in order to fulfill our combine will!

THE POLICE FORCE

The police literally means- law enforcement; keep watch over, community monitors- The police are normal individuals brought together, organized, and trained to guard and guide the masses to the rule of law and order as enshrined in their national constitution.

The police force comprises of men and women with the discipline to harness their combined energy to enforce and maintain the current laws of each government; wherever, whenever and however they are assigned to represent them; for the smooth and harmonious dispensation of law and justice, and for the benefit of the people of that given country or state.

In the present order of things, the entire police force will need reshuffling in order to embrace this new concept aimed at rechanneling the affairs of this nation and the entire world.

In addition, to do all that as well as give credence to this new concept of policing:

-All the present national activities of the police will have to be controlled and directed by one central body, which will be devised and established by the ex-NIPH students; must be founded by only men and women of highest integrity and humanitarian consciousness, people with deep fear of God and respect for life and creatures.

- Every given offence or an infringement of any law of the people, the culprit should be judged with the customary law of the community or local council in where the said offence took place. Their rulings and decisions should be streamlined with and reflect the general constitution of the federated nation in fairness and good spirit.

-The police forces will have to be retrained to quench riots of various dimensions; acts of indiscipline and vandalism without the use of mortal weapons. And if they have to carry and use any weapon, it should only serve to immobilize culprits for couple of hours without killing or do serious damage or harm to any individual; enough of unnecessary killings and intimidation. No one in this world has any right to kill others, you are not God; enough…

-Each nation or region will continue to enjoy the protection and services of indigenous men and women under the system name- **'community-policing'** which will be organized and controlled through the mandate of a **'Global Police Headquarters'** or **national police headquarters** in this case; that will be duly established in the nearest future.

-We cannot rely on the hope that everyone will consciously do things right; but we strongly belief that this policies will help to mitigate the majority of the negative conducts streaming in the veins of a good number of humankind.

-The police should possess the grand responsibility for operating and policing the rest of the governmental organs, including the public. They will police the incumbent leaders; the public, financial institutions, schools, religious bodies and the department of justice etcetera.

-The Police should possess the common sense to persuade everyone to keep and obey those laws and orders with a reasonable deep sense of patriotism.

-Offenders under this new system of things will have to face, not an arbitrary judge or judgment but a kind of judgment dispensed by "The Community Law Keepers", who will be elected through unanimous decisions from within each region or community.

"The Community Law Keepers"- will have the authority to represent and reflect the common feelings of a given community where the said offence took place; and with due consideration for what brought about the offence; dish out a fair and humane judgment.

What Type of Judicial and Security System would be Most Appropriate for this New Ideology and What Will Duly Relieve the Heavy Security Burden on the Police Force?

- I will suggest for a judicial system similar to that of the 'Crown Court' as is being practiced in the UK. Each regional community will have only one or two Crown Courts depending on population and size of the region. Every Crown Court will have to be presided over by a local legal representative appointed from the 'National judicial headquarters'. The national judicial headquarters will be solely responsible for making final decision on all judicial affairs such as: appointing Crown Court judges, hearing of all Appeal Cases, and establishment of Crown Courts wherever due.

-The tasks for the Crown Courts will be to ratify and seal the decisions made by the jury members if found to streamline within the arm of love, peace and harmony.

-Some minor offences can be resolved and dealt with at the local jury levels; but the more serious cases that may hinder mass peace and tranquility should be forwarded to the judicial headquarters for appropriate deliberation.

-Justice should be allowed to proceed smoothly without fear or favor; it should always aim to ascertain that no single individual be ever or often victimized in any given circumstance, just as is common in this present judicial dispensation.

-Every case should be listened to attentively, examined without bias or prejudice; and not only basing judgments on face value or the horrors of an offence committed. Best approach should be to lay more emphasis on reasons and motives behind every presumed offense committed. It is natural for people to react over matters affecting them according to their personal conceptions, convictions and impulses inherent from culture or birth.

-Therefore, in any breach of the laws of the community or nation, the members of the duly established jury should always endeavor to put themselves in the position of the offender so as to understand the ulterior motive behind the offense or offender.

If the reaction of the culprit over the committed offense is of a natural human reaction, by putting into consideration how majority of us could react under such a situation, pardon and forgiveness should be granted and the person cautioned to desist from further misdemeanors or actions that could create discord in the community.

-If found that the motive for the offense was based on intentional aggravation or self-defense, the culprit will be allowed to go home or given the most minimum sentence possible; irrespective of the gravity of offense committed- that should be the aim of justice; and not to take things too personal; setting people up as examples, for others to see how mean and fearful the law can be, no! the rule of divine justice is to teach, not condemn.

-For offenses without enough evidence, the accused should be given the benefit of doubt; case dismissed and the culprit admonished and pleaded with, to sin no more.

-The community or state should never try to condemn anyone when the offense accused of is not beyond reasonable doubt.

-All the national and global human communities should be sensitized and made to know that their security and their judicial balance is in their respective hands and should as a matter of patriotism, report always, any act of indiscipline or misconduct witnessed within their communities to report them to the appropriate body or police in charge of that region.

-It is not appropriate for people to let things around them go wrong while they wait for the government or police to figure and fix things for everyone by themselves alone. It's your problem; your community problem is your personal problem; see it that way always and do something about it within your individual abilities within the rule in our constitution.

-The system is for all and never for those in power alone. If everyone helps to control crime and fight injustice and indiscipline, things will surely function a lot better for all and then help to ease the heavy burden on security and social peace and harmony levied upon the police or other armed forces.

-If the national or global community could find a way to curb and reduce or eradicate wicked crimes through persuasion, collective initiatives or individual volition, the lawyers then will have no need for their present jobs. Therefore, can go into other sectors or more lucrative businesses of their choices or try to convert their collective talents into other sectors of public services more profitable to humanity. A similar situation will face the prison workers and those indirectly or directly dependent on penitentiary and judicial arm of the government.

-Imagine the amount of money and manpower to be saved which can better be invested into agricultural researches and food production. If only for example we are able to peacefully do away with prisons and criminal lawyers; because there is peace, love and harmony vibrating out of every of our regional and global communities! All the criminal lawyers, prison warders and prison inmates voluntarily becoming food producers and caretakers of things of Creation! I will live to see that day come to reign!

However, the ex-NIPH students will find a better way to harness all such such delicate issues of mutual benefit for all communities within their habitat…

TAXES OR TAXATION

-No More Taxes on People or Properties Henceforth-

Taxes for whatever purposes they may serve or have been serving up until now, should come to an immediate end. Taxes on people income or properties should be discouraged henceforth; be nullified and prohibited. Working and paying for our services is more than enough for an each individual to be allowed total control over their properties or earnings! Forced taxation is a criminal act in the spiritual realm!

There should be no more taxes of any kind whether from individuals, companies, organizations or properties. People should be encouraged to work freely, learn freely and manage freely the wages of their sweats without any form of intrusion.

-The Funds for any government project should come from the numerous natural resources endowed upon the nations of the world by the Creator. Out of that, they (the governing body) should pay salaries for their employees, create jobs and save for projects intended for social development. On the other hand, each person has a natural responsibility to create and fend for him or her.

-Taxation on people's efforts and proceeds have the uncanny feel and connotation of oppression and suppression- anything that is done by force and with coercion can never make anyone happy. – inflicting in others such ugly feelings of obligation, makes them feel victimized, and such acts are against the spirit of this new order of things! Taking money from the 'have-nots', does not make a good impression irrespective of how genuine your reasons maybe for doing so.

-It is very ugly when mentors, teachers or guardians who are supposed to cater and nurture their supposed children, start asking – rather forcing their children: to pay money to them as TAX because they work; to pay because they feed, to pay because they live in a house or to pay because their vehicles apply on tarred roads which were naturally meant for all to use; etcetera.

The act of taxation on the general public, seen from the humane point of view of the order of the things of natural creation, gives the same ugly impression like of those from abusive parents who intentionally send their young and fragile children out to the street to work and beg for alms while they stay home: eating, drinking, laughing and waiting for their children to return with food and money as to support them; and at the very expense of their children's well-being; subjecting their very young and famished children to undue hardship and uncertainty. For this very reason and many more, taxation has to be deleted from our respective national lexicons!

What Should Replace Direct Taxes on People and Properties?

-In place of direct taxes on people and properties, the ex-NIPH students will have to set up a central national body with representatives from all over the regions of the nations who shall be fully in charge of collecting voluntary donations from the general public – they can apply the same tactics used by the religious organizations; in this way the governing body should be able to receive regular assistance from the public; also, the national populace should be sensitized on the regular need to or whenever possible, as a matter of national duty, contribute to the established organization in all regions.

-The said organization in return, will be responsible for sponsoring all government and public projects; sponsor also, individual talents and ideas that shall benefit the general public when accomplished.

-The said organization should also collaborate with all the financial institutions in the loaning of money and financial assistance to the general public that are genuinely in need of the money and with a viable project that will pay back the loan without interest or with a token for the back payment.

-The banking industry will be reviewed- in fact, bankers should come together and find other ways to encourage people to manage their money in a way that discourages using cash and liquid money; and discourage also, robbers and bums, who see the banking industry as a gateway to quick and easy money.

My Piece of Advice to All the Nations and to the Global Community as one:

-Fervently living and following the natural laws of creation at all times and in all things, I have come to discover this natural fact that, people will voluntarily give away nearly all they own to support a just cause; be it national or personal cause, better than when they are reminded or forced to give their hard-earned effort away over shady causes. This is going to be the new global attitude towards all things concerning humankind. Stop forcing people to do things they are not comfortable with; things they refuse to consent to…

-We should try to give total power and rely strongly on the day-to-day running of the affairs of the society to the: Police, the Community Jury, the Funding Organizations and above all to the News Media Outlets who should be proactive in the campaign for unity, exemplary actions and sense of cohesion instead of conspiratorial, sensational and fake news reports; we will have no more need for all that in this new dispensation; renaissance.

-I will suggest that the News Media should have a complete freedom of expression. They are the –**"community, national and all-seeing-Global-Eyes"** They should work hand-in-hand with the Police force; thus, globalizing the News Media and stopping the present system of selling information meant to educate or enlighten the public as things are happening and without adding or removing.

-People should stop buying and selling information; education and information should be as free as the air that we breathe.

This is because, the ultimate pleasure that can be derived from or out of any experience or acquired knowledge, is only in the **act of sharing** those experiences with others and that is what we intend to do in this present order of things. The news media, the police and similar public servants should receive salaries from the United Funding Body, which will be set up on a national and global dimension.

The national or global News Media should always offer: free services, completely free and fair information dissemination!

Our communities, our nations and world in general will definitely get much better if we can adopt and implement these few strategies in our respective ruling constitutions; let our constitutions be founded on openness, fairness, empathy and transparency; then and only then, we can joyfully embrace unity, peace and balanced progress in all our neighborhood.

SCHOOL AND SCHOOLING

-Self-Education- the Best Natural System of Acquiring Knowledge and Wisdom-

The main aim for school and schooling is certainly for easy and synchronized indoctrination of the public for the benefit of all through: mutual communication and global collaboration!

School is an institution of learning where different subjects are being taught and imparted at various levels, for the main purpose of making as many people as possible to know the same thing and think in the same way. The main aim being to help us uniformly apply the acquired discipline or knowledge whenever and wherever the need may arise within the periphery of our collective national or global community; be it in the far future or in the immediate present.

-The above views into consideration, the ex-NIPH students will review the entire academic systems for the kind of subjects being imparted to children and adults as well; and classify them according to their level of importance or benefit to the combined society of humankind.

Subjects such as: biology, chemistry, physics, mathematics, geography etcetera with universal formulae should be allowed to continue to be taught in schools to at least a basic level, after undergoing major rewriting; that is because they bear laws and formulae that have been helpful to humankind to bind things of imagination and creation together since time immemorial; and, for the enhancement of technological advancement which is considered a necessity for our collective wellbeing now and in the future to come.

-The other subjects can be optional. People should study at leisure and in harmony with their natural potentials avoiding any kind of obligation or coercion on any subject matter.

-Such subjects as: religion, history, sociology and archaeology etcetera are alright to be made optional as school or as academic subjects so as to keep such subjects alive. These subjects could be encouraged through documentaries, movies, televisions and computer programs for everyone to see and know about their past and spiritual values, especially, the growing children who will still need to know their history and origin.

-Work and rewards should be based on individual abilities, determination and willingness to work and learn to do a given job; and not putting into consideration the level of education or studies carried out or attained by an individual. I see it more appropriate to reward the level of experience, dedication to a particular profession or job than the level of academic education acquired. People should avoid being in a hurry to do or finish a given job, attain fame and to make money or material aggrandizement; it is more rewarding instead, to aim to do your respective best and to do most of the things correctly streamlined within your natural pace of life.

-Education or academic studies are in the same category as physical exercises and games; they are both personal initiatives to better one through doing something, which one is talented in or passionate about and should therefore be free of choice.

-I feel that the level of education as well as political engagements should not be the basis for economic rewards above the real work done or output in positive services to others; good services deserve bigger reward in economic or otherwise.

- Teachers, Media men and women, authors and writers of various categories should be paid, pampered for their respective contributions in educating and disseminating information that so much help to motivate the general public towards sound and good behaviors that help to promote national or global peace and harmony. That is to say that we should henceforth begin to reward positive contributions as a way to encourage more people doing good services to others, instead of rewarding academic achievements and degrees obtained from schools of learning. And desists from making fake heroes off people through inflated news broadcast

-Every time someone starts a business, whether funded by the "Funding Body" or not, if that person chooses to hire extra work force as done by companies or big businesses,the employee or workers should be paid by the employers through the Central Funding Body' who in turn will pay those workers according to the existing service norms.

The business owners should pay themselves with the money they make from their businesses and owe no allegiance whatsoever to anyone except to those who work for them. The only spiritual obligation being that business owners should once in a while give regular tithe or donations to the Funding Body' which they should honestly use for projects aimed at social and technological development of the given region.

If humankind could be able to bring them to consciously practice and execute all of the above, things of this world shall certainly begin to improve for the better. Otherwise, on the contrary, humanity as a whole will be busy singing alleluia, clapping hands in praise to the lord, keeping night vigils in churches and at home, accumulating academic degrees, knocking and bashing their heads on stones and floors in prayers, starve themselves to death in the name of the unseen Creator, and all that will be to no gain.

Trust me, my fellow humans! Upon doing all that prayers and fasting, you will still find yourselves millions of miles still far away from the Promised Land. Not only that, you will find yourselves retrogressing miles away rather than miles forward to this promised land or truth in other words, which is the ultimate desire of everyone!

Crime and violence will continue to multiply inflicting on all humankind like stings from the bees. Disease will be ravaging people in large numbers. Hunger and misery will painfully be sucking your blood and flesh like the leeches.

Fear, terror and insecurity will dominate this world keeping everyone scared and unsure of the next day if it comes or not; and suffocate any trace of meaningful joy, peace and pleasure in your respective lives!

Schools, schooling and academic education are good attributes to acquire; but, please let every human know that, true education is not that in which one is encouraged by relatives to embark upon. It is pursuing that in which, you are naturally inclined. The most educated people are not those who went through the academic walls, but those who know where and how to get whatever they need to realize their set-goals in life and in harmony; without violating anyone's right. We go to school because we feel it is best to; in the same way we can do very well without school if all things were allowed to remain equal. Knowledge is not locked within the walls of school or established institution.

Humans are meant to be curious, and curiosity happens to be the nucleus or foundation of inventions. Be naturally curious, ask yourselves questions, ask your parents questions, ask your God questions and analyze their answer; then make your choices and seek and to find. The world is for you, the living, make good use of your given potentials and live the best of it.

In truth, no human being owes any form of obligation towards another; the only two entities you are intrinsically obliged to respond to or give account of every step of your life to, are who? You and your Creator; particularly to yourself and due in respect to others and things…

WORK AND WORKING

-Five-Hour Work per day for all Citizens-

-Work and working for all humanity from today should be evaluated in, and streamlined into-**Labors of Love and Joy- We need** to work in harmony with our nature, for the most part, for the benefit of others; and for others to work for our benefit in return. That is sharing, and sharing multiplies earnings and spreads- love and happiness. That is in harmony with one of the nature's laws. The theme and work norm should be "working for each other and not, others working for you" No one should work for no one, we should join hands to work for each other; that is the nature's rules that enhances positive and balanced progress.

-The more you are able to give in service to others, the more you receive physically, spiritually and materially in return. Do not underestimate these principles of life!

- The Creator, our God had for long designed and laid down the basic and ultimate works which is necessary to keep Earth life in continues revolution, evolution and devolution or fading-out.

-Every human should bear in mind that we have no part to play in the creation of anything new.-Our only work is to live-out our lives in harmony with things of nature; within our vicinity. The other things you may import or refine are complimentary to things that are or were.

-Just like our Dogs; Horses, Chicken or even the Insects lives out their lives in harmony with the ordinance sof nature, we should consciously imitate or copy from other animals we know. They radiate peace and harmony wherever they find themselves at any given moment in time.

However, for humans, they always want to recreate out of that which had been created; fantasize and analyze things that they see or hear about.

-Humans being among the weakest and feeblest of all the creatures are driven by fear of death; thus, they spend their entire time on earth in search of security through: arms, food, clothes, housing; it is just a pure human nature. There is nothing wrong with our human nature; but, to consolidate our lives, we must know, understand our human nature and our driving forces…

-Humans, as all other creatures are structured to survive independently of any external assistance other than with the natural materials provided to them within the vicinity of their respective habitat.

-Working yourself to exhaustion is a sign of ignorance, fear and frustration. You should know that in your entire efforts to make your lives and the world better as you say, you are only working against the wind. As a result, you are rather obstructing the natural course of things of creation, and, therefore generate conflicting energy forces against the natural configuration of our creator who whom we war against each to worship and adore.

-Know that all our frenetic human efforts to challenge the immutable forces of nature tantamount to shadow-pursuit and vanity; end of the road is what you are destined to meet. To know what is behind the end of the road, you will have to gear up to go for it in accord concordance with the subtle realities of our entire nature as humans…

- Do not take yourselves very serious because your life and the act of living are meant to be a thing of pleasure and not that of war and mare fruitless laboring.

-Try to give much time to yourself in meditation, contemplation, appreciation, physical and mental exercises; the rest of your time should be shared between the joyful work you decide to do, and the people around you; with nature as your source of energy.

-Doing these is the same as, living in harmony with nature, in peace as a creature in nature and not living in continuous confrontation against the Creator or as the creator yourself.

-We should understand the paramount importance, the benefit we receive when we share and enjoy with each other than when we manipulate and hate each other. When we do not share our knowledge and work with each other, we automatically encourage us to live negatively with no advantage or sustainable benefit. This is not what we intend to earn from life, or is it?

-Work is the act of expending ones energy to realize a synchronized activity with the aim to achieve economic, material or spiritual benefit for the growth and betterment of oneself, others and the things of creation within the entire eco-system.

-Working is a necessary exercise from nature for the purpose of refurbishing and fortifying the degenerative tissues of human muscles and organs, with the main aim to regularly maintain a sound and healthy body. For this, all forms of work should be felt as a medium to feel pleasure; contrarily, any act or work that fails to give or provide pleasurable conditions, is not good enough for you and should not be continued for long. Work you do not like should be done for some time in order to get to what you like and need. Our system of leadership should be very mindful of this simple but, effective part of human nature.

-Whenever you engage in any job or work that does not give a pleasurable sensation; the time given to that working hours is wasted due to the fact that the inherent pleasure of doing a thing is being denied. The work becomes a source of torture instead of a source of pleasure. To be happy with what you do or are doing, you must have the desire from deep down within to it for self convincing reason.

-But on the contrary, when we engage in work that we like and enjoy doing, this triggers a pleasurable sensation, which aids psychological and physical healthiness that also, motivates one to give out in services one's very best; and this state of mind, is the basis and essence of all human achievements, it stimulates sound mental force and positive growth.

-That is the main spirit behind all the wonders ever performed by humankind in this world you and I live in today as people also lived it in the past.

- All that we see and assume as technology and great works of art are based on works of passion executed by people motivated out of difficulties or inspirations, beliefs and faith in the things they do.

-Therefore, we should learn to engage in jobs that we like and enjoy doing.

-We should also try to employ people in jobs that they show natural inclination or penchant for; and should avoid doing a job, just for the money and material benefits they offer. When you do things you are not inclined to by your nature, you only open your door ajar for depression and unhappiness to work in and out of your awesome life. Desist from doing so; through planning and Thought-Sequence you can discover your real and actual talents.

-Look around you and you are sure to see depression and weak looking people all around you; have you ever stopped to ask why much sadness around you? Stressed and depressive moods are most common nowadays-in places of work; and why most people are daily yielding less and less off their natural potentials. The simple reason is because they are not doing what they love doing!

-This new system of doing things should encourage majority of our citizens to work more for themselves at their own comfortable times of the day or night without limitations and obligations of any type whatsoever. This is the only justifiable way to make majority of our citizens to inculcate the good habit of going the extra-mile at all times and in every form of work, they engage in. Is there any working adult who does not know the horrors of working for a boss; or the joy of working for oneself at one's own schedule?

-The fact is that whenever we work for ourselves especially, in activities we like, we tend to work for much longer. In addition, it is more rewarding. For this very reason, we feel it is better to change the old working conditions to make work for every global citizen, a thing of joy; instead of a thing of torture and constant agony. Given that, we have to spend our entire lifetime doing that- working. To work is one of the rules of nature, and obligation of inherent from birth; and, the moment you stop working hard and happy, that very moment you will start to die and atrophy without knowing it!

-All the money and material wealth cannot save you or reverse that law of our nature –That We Shall Eat with the Work We Do- as it is for the wretched and poor, so, it is for the strong and rich. No one can escape physical and mental exercises or challenges for long and remain healthy. Both the poor and the rich! So love the jobs you do and work with joy and enthusiasm for the sake of serenity, peace and harmony!

RETIREMENT SCHEME

-No More Job Retirement for all Citizens-

What is retirement?

Retirement is withdrawal or giving up of work from active services to the public. Retirement is simply, to give up doing work for the people especially, when under the government services of which everyone who works legally will do at the long run!

-The question is what is the rationale or real meaning of retiring or giving up active work or services for one and for others?

-What should a healthy person do if he/she stops to work for himself or serve others? Should they sleep away the rest of their remaining lifetime; embark on roaming aimlessly around the world in search of pleasure/adventure; or better still, live and rot in any small Island sunbathing, as is done in these recent times? Are these the best ways to find joy, good health and happiness that we all desire and work hard for?

-Know it that, our respective human mind and body has imbued rules and regulations embodied in them right from our birth and from our creation. Our body and mind feed and grow better through effective and active use of it and on the contrary, they atrophy, deteriorate and fade-off faster than it was designed to be!

-For those very reasons, *people to retire from active work or services for themselves and to others are synonymous to sealing your spiritual death warrant! Because, it is one of nature's rules that, each time you give out anything whatsoever, automatically you will receive in proportion to that given and the moment you stop giving, you also seize to receive in equal proportion to that not given out or shared!*

-When you voluntarily retire from an active job or service, you can be compensated with money or material rewards, but, the fundamental which is your spiritual needs cannot be paid for with any material rewards; but, can only be reached and acquired through the dint of hard or soft mind and body work…

The human mind is a natural organ, which readily adheres only to the specifics of nature's ethics and dictates without remorse; but, cannot fully respond to human influences or manipulations without a negative consequence. Therefore, human mind knows not the meaning of such things as time, age, years, today, and tomorrow etcetera. Worst still, retirement. You cannot carry over the joy, pleasure, or pain of this moment to another day or another moment. Human mind or spirit does not function with the tangibles but rather functions best with the intangibles. If our human mind or life were to function well with riches and material possessions, I feel almost all people in America and Europe should be the happiest people on earth; but are they?

As I write this piece, I live not more than thirty meters to the sea with my family in the South of Tenerife, Canary Island of Spain. I assure you, ninety percent of my neighbors are retired people from all parts of what you refer to as 'civilized world': Germans, British, Italians, Swedish, French etcetera. In reality, entire Canary Island is nearly constructed and built as it is today, mostly out of the money from these retirees and subventions from other sources.

Apart from those who visit the Island daily for few weeks on holiday, most of the retirees actually own their dream houses here in the Island. Most live in absolute human comfort. but, what struck me most was, seeing the high degree of spiritual and physical deterioration amongst these retired people; most of them are invalids, others who are well look so wrinkled and worn-out that all the best food and money in this world cannot fix them back anymore...

I also know that, nearly all or most of those people had worked or served their nations in various fields for nothing less than thirty and forty years of their respective youthful lives; some must have worked in extreme weather conditions such as snow in hope and wait for these retirement days.

Understand that to live a balanced and worthy life, a reasonable amount of positive-energy is required without which money and all the material possessions become worthless to you that instant.

My grandfather died at the sound age of hundred and five years (105 yrs), he was already eighty-four years old (84 yrs) by the time I was born. Irrespective of that, I can assure you, as I write this, after having travelled, worked and lived in nearly all the continents in this world, I have never met people with the kind of energy and what I refer to as a Good and Positive Life; as I witnessed in my grandpa; and in those of his generation. My grandmother as well lived for ninety-eight-years (98 years) but, I can assure you that those people never had social security protections, never received pensions money, never had doctors and nurses catering to them neither could they read or write, but they had everything in abundance from 'Mother-Nature' what do you think about that? Is Mother Nature being unfair or are we the responsible architects of our personal and collective challenges?

At their later age, my grandpa and grandma used to walk bare-foot for over two-three kilometers all day to their vast farms for work and back home when they were tired; eat and rest well, make fiestas, attend to community meetings, visit friends and be visited by friends with constant entertainment at all times of the day or night.

At the end, they had everything in excess. I saw them constantly sharing food and all things among themselves with joy, unity and respect for each other; for Mother Nature and the culture that bind them together.

Certainly, I have never seen or lived with similar love, peace and harmony, which I had the privilege to witness few years ago ever since I left that environment and that generation!

It is a big shame and disappointment that despite all our present progress and development we still are unable to achieve such sense of love, peace and harmony in consonance with the good old days. That was the only period of my life which, I still hold in- Highest Esteem till date and obviously forever because nothing foreseeable is going to replace the inborn divine wisdom from past ancestors.

During those periods, I learnt more natural lifestyle, ways of living natural that I really enjoyed and tried to retain while making effort to separate reality with their numerous superstitious beliefs very rampant of that era.

The only thing they did well in those days that sustained them so well, I believe was that, they simply adhered in harmony and respect to Mother Nature; they flowed with the tide instead of going against it as we are doing today in all our obsessive efforts to negatively and forcefully challenge and work against our 'Beloved Mother Nature' and in contravention of creational rules of the Creator.

RECOMMENDATION

-In this context, I would suggest that we allow people to work or give their services to themselves and their communities willingly as far as, and in as much as they are able to without problems and excess bureaucratic obstacles.

-We should employ people in only jobs they like to do especially those in which we notice that they have the natural flair for it.

-instead of retiring our advanced and experienced workers, we should do best by forming or establishing a **'National and Global Association for 'Advanced-Workers'** spread-out to cover every field of endeavor; that will give them the collective chance to continue to impart and impact their years of experiences on the growing generation. That will serve both partie much better and lucrative than rendering them and their years of experiences null and void through outright retirement.

 In this way, our advanced-parents will continue to feel useful and helpful to the youth and to the society in general. This is going to as well encourage their mind to continue to give and receive than to surrender and reduce or become marginalized down the brinks of the society which they just started constructing years back...

-no matter how little anyone's mind is able to function, if that mind is connected to the cord of positive mental attitude, as physically handicapped that person maybe, the mind can still do great things and achieve awesome results which could benefit that person and others in no small measures.

-we should stop making life easy for ourselves without struggle or efforts, because, doing so, is utterly inimical to sound health and good living in the long run.

-Let us confront old age without fear and worry; instead of fear and apprehension, accept it with serenity and as natural as part of the processes of life and living; Period!

-No need to panic and fret about what will happen to us at old age and when we are sick; what you fear most comes to you eventually; this notion conforms to nature's rule.

-Stop worrying and be happy and plan better for that is all you owe to yourself, the world and to the Creator; period!

CELEBRATION AND FIESTA

-Compulsory Celebration Days' for all Citizens-

Celebrations and merriment are the best aspect of human existence. The feeling derived out of celebrations is the only human feeling that cannot be faked; that breaks all barriers, permits no limitations for genders, creed or origin. It is the most encompassing human feeling of all time; the most positive human endowment which unites one with oneself, others and the unseen spirits. Celebrations are hearty food for the souls of every living and non-living things. Each Fiesta is a lubricant to the human bones and joints; body builder and brain cleanser…so let us celebrate at all times!

We should celebrate every day that we are alive to rekindle the sunlight in us at all times. Such feelings or emotions should be part of our daily affairs; we should map out time for celebrations or fiestas everyday as we do with all other things; don't you agree?

We should endeavor to stop the tendency to suffocate the good feelings manifesting out of us, which we refer to as happiness so we can enjoy our lives to the fullest possible without stepping on other's toes or infringe on the sources of wellbeing.

-Does it make sense to wait to celebrate Christmas; New Year, birthdays and all such occasion when we could rightly celebrate every moment of our lives? All things being equal and there is no cogent reason why we cannot celebrate every given day in our lives!

-Know that, in as much as it is nice to celebrate occasions such as: Christmas, birthdays, new year's etc. such acts or moments duly create unnecessary stress to the brain, while all you really sort after is nothing other than: simple momentary joy, pleasure and serenity of mind and body at all possible moments. Surely, there is nothing wrong with celebrating; New Years, Christmas, Birthday parties etc. those occasions are great and marvelous to celebrate, but they are best celebrated often in order for us to regularly savor the positive energy that can be derived from such celebrations and feasting.

-Regularity, punctuality with sincerity of purpose is traits that evenly create warm wave of harmony or vitality in our brain cells. When we feast or celebrate, we feel good and important; so, why not therefore celebrate and feast more than you often labor in and for vain pursuits and values?

Naturally, do you think it's best to postpone, prolong and wait too long to celebrate and feast while the rest of our days dwindle in hardship and sadness? Give your answers and reasons if you have them!

Nevertheless, if for any reason we are unable to schedule and fix -National and Global Days for Mass Celebration and Feasting- then that duty will go under the umbrella of the ex-NIPH students who will be duly trained to think and reason in the best interest of the people they pilot to this unknown destination of life's journey. Instead of the present system of what you can get from and out of the people; leaders are servants to the people and not the other way round.

FOOD AND FEEDING

-Good Eating Habit for all Citizens-

Food serves to regenerate and revitalize the tissues and the body organs among other-substances of benefit. Food is any substance especially solid or liquid taken into the body and assimilated by cells for the purpose of growth, nourishment of the body and the mind.

Food with air and water are the fundamental ingredients for life; no Food, water and Air, no life! The entire living creatures: Humans, animals and plants need food on a daily basis to continue living. All the energy they will need to activate the smooth functioning of their entire body organs for: moving, eating, talking, etc is derived from food and feeding. No one can live for long without ingesting food and water.

-Notwithstanding, many have adopted what we refer to as 'bad eating habits' – eating at random times without allowing previously eaten meals complete the ongoing digestion process in the intestines; and also, eating and indulging excessively harms in equal or more proportion.

-The negative habit of eating at random also tamper with the purpose for food intake. It is worthy for people to know and understand that, it is neither an obligation nor necessary to eat three square meals daily in order to remain healthy and happy.

-Food like other things of creation has both negative and positive effects. The same food, as nice and as life saving as they can be, is also, among the top killers in this nation of people and animals. Most of the known diseases that usually attack humans come from food-intake; imagine the unfriendly odor of rotten or spoilt food; your feces or excrement; the acidity in your urine; imagine how disgusting those can be to your sense of smell! Therefore, good health and happy living is not about how much you eat but how well you can manage and rationalize your habit to food intake.

Everything about life and humans will always yield better results when done with discipline and in a balanced state of mind. Eventually, with self-discipline in most cases some of us discover ways to eat correctly and appropriately by adopting at will, what we refer to as 'a good eating habit'.

A balanced person listens to the ways his/her body reacts to every food intake and unconsciously records the feelings he or she usually obtains after eating. This is because everything that concerns humanity in relation to his growth, is constantly noted or experienced through the aid of the intangibles known as 'Feelings', 'Taste', Smell' and 'Sight etc.

-To eat healthy in accord with ones unique taste or 'gusto' there is the need to listen to the 'feel'; how you feel after eating whatever it is that you have eaten. You should keep taking note of your favorite food intakes; relying on how your body system assimilates or rejects it. By doing that, and with time you will arrive at a sound selection of food that your body system will always like most, digest and assimilates better. When you are able to achieve that, keep feeding on those kinds of food for as long as your body-systems continue to like and accept them.

-Never eat because others are eating or force yourself to eat at the time they do if your body will not be comfortable with the food at that moment; it is not wise to eat such things or those foodstuffs that cause discomfort to your digestive systems.

-Always allow enough time in between meals; eat only when you are really hungry and not because there is food and it looks appetizing.

-Learn to eat very sparingly; always empty your bowels every morning before the first meal of the day and brush your teeth as many times as you may deem necessary.

-You should in reality brush your teeth and tongue each time you smell rotten food in your mouth and that should be as many times as necessary- mostly whenever you eat any dairy products, chocolate and sugary stuff.

-Most people do not care much for their teeth and breathe. All they care to do is eat, drink and smoke without maintaining the organs that make eating possible – teeth, tongue, mouth, and stomach as a whole should be the part of the body organs that we need to treat with utmost respect and care; plus, 'bowel cleansing' through regular and daily excretion.

-Know that to eat healthy does not mean to eat more, worst of all is eating randomly.

-There is nothing more troublesome for the body than eating at all times- suffocating the metabolic system without allowing it adequate time to complete the digestion process before pumping down more food into the stomach.

-If you eat too much or too little, your body system will equally react negatively.

Your main job as humans is to find, always, the balance in any venture at all times.

-Punctuality and regularity; these are two of the positive ingredients of universal life. Nature does not give much room for over-indulgence; over-indulgence weakens the soul and suffocates willpower.

-Every human that eats must as a matter of universal duty and obligation, be able to contribute in food production or at least in creative ventures while living.

-Every human is supposed to produce their own food and shelter if all things should remain equal; or left in conformity with creational rules; devoid of manipulation and adulteration; people could and should be the captain of their given lives. Food energizes the enter body and empowers thought process.

Research and learn to cater for your lovely-self more than any other thing or person!

SEX AND SEXUAL ORGANS

-Teach Sex and Sexual Organs to all Citizens-

Sexual organs are the most fundamental human body organs; the male and female sex-organs: Mr. Penis and Mrs. Vagina are jointly responsible for all the pleasures and upheavals pervading the entire ecosystem; they proliferate the world with human geniuses and idiots, strong and weak, good and bad. Without Mr. Penis and Mrs. Vagina there will be no more people to continue with the affairs of this world just after the last set dies and fade-out.

Many do not freely talk about sexual issues with joy and appreciation. These magnificent organs are rather treated with scorn; as dirty and should always be kept secret or sacred. Sacred; it is acceptable and appropriate for Mr. Penis and Mrs. Vagina to be felt and treated as *"SACRED BODY ORGANS!"*

I think it is stupid for us to be adorned with such important and indispensable organs and yet, not use them freely with joy and pride for which they are duly worth.

The female oval shaped sexual organ biologically known as Vagina; and the rocket or bullet-shaped male sexual organ similarly known as Penis, are the two most important human organs after the heart and a sound brain. Through them we are able to urinate without which we will rut in deadly complications; through the combined actions of the two opposite sexual organs, we are able to consummate sexual intercourse which results in pregnancy and child-bearing; and of course aiding the continuity of species and their races, without which there will be a definite extinction of all created creature within few decades!

We must therefore try to respect our sexual desires with love and affection and do make honest effort to consummate our respective sexual-drive in freedom, gratitude and appreciation.

The ex-NIPH students will find a most acceptable way for the public to talk about and treat 'sex-matters' in a way to remove the taboos and prejudices attached to sexual consummation and the sex-organs. I suggest we must exclude the irrational talks of morality and religious sentiments attached to people's sexual feelings.

Parents owe a grand duty to teach their respective children the true functions of sex and sexual organs, with natural and open mind; and without the present sense of bias, shame or guilt which had from the past, erroneously attached to our most important organs – sex organs-.

Sex is a word with many definitions: it could simply refer to the two muscular organs located between the two thighs, at the lower part of the body used for urinating and sexual gratification for male genders; and for the female genders, apart from urinating and sexual gratification, their sex organs are also used for child bearing and menstruation. 'Sex' as a word could also be used to refer to individual gender: femininity for female sex organ; masculinity for male sex organ.

But here, in this book, the word sex will be used to refer to the act of copulation: introducing the male's warm and erect penis into the female's warm, soft and oval shaped vagina with the aim of realizing sexual gratification between both of them. This very act of copulation or sexual gratification is being wrongly sought after between men and women of varying age groups.

The gratification or pleasure derived from sexual intercourse between a man and a woman is most of the times so deep and satisfying that many people crazily search for it in uncontrolled manners, thereby making the act, very inimical to the senses of equilibrium and mental balance.

Many people as a result also, have resorted to taking advantage of their sexual organs for economic gains through practicing of such things as prostitution, raping, pornography etc.

These days, it had become very trendy to commercialize and abuse sex under various socially accepted names such as:

homosexuality – the act of having intercourse between man and man or woman and woman instead of the natural way which is between a man and a woman for the main aim of reproduction and multiplication of our human population for the purpose of continuity.

- **Prostitution** – the act of accepting money or any other form of material gains in order to have sex or make love.

-**Pornography** – the act of allowing oneself to be recorded making love to oneself (referred to as masturbation) or to another with the final aim of material gains or aggrandizement.

-**Rape**– the act of having sexual relation with another by applying force or violence; which in most cases, ends up in brutal killing, kidnapping, and even mutilation of the body of the raped.

However, let it be known that the main functions of the sex organs are:

-To derive pleasure in love making between a man and a woman

- To urinate.

-To menstruate and finally:

-To bear children. Any other thing is considered immorality or sexual abuse to most men and the Creator!

The only acceptable sexual conduct in the sight of God and man is an intercourse carried out under the influence of love; provoked by going through the gradual processes of courtship and courtesy in bid to lure or conquer the opposite sex to willingly succumb to sexual consummation between them. This kind of sexual gratification must be preceded by communication, admiration, and respect and with abundant kisses intermingled with deepest feelings.

In this premise, for any marital relationship to be considered successful, adequate and satisfactory sexual intercourse must remain a fundamental factor because it is very necessary to lubricate the 'tensions and chains' of daily human survival challenges.

Well consumed sexual intercourse carried out with deep love and affection is a sound mental and physical elixir. It is on the other hand also a panacea to: stress, depression and dissatisfaction – so go for it ladies and gentlemen but, with good intents and moderation!

I would encourage the world to take love, sex and sexual intercourse as seriously as the food that we eat and air that we breathe.

Forced sexual intercourse does not give real satisfaction to any sane human. In a similar way, when children are born out of deep love, they usually live and behave with much mental balance and maturity throughout their life cycle; willingly accepting everything about this world with admiration, respect and appreciation. On the contrary, even the parents of such children born without deep and harmonious sex affairs are usually found wanton in the way they behave both as kids and as adults and their conducts are usually unpredictable.

Therefore, sexual intercourse with a loving heart and sexual intercourse without a loving heart, which will you favor most and encourage? Send out your answers and comments!

EXERCISES

-Mind and Body Exercise Must Be Mandatory for all Citizens-

What is Exercise?

Exercise is the voluntary or involuntary act of engaging the body and soul in activities that heat up the muscles and organs causing the heart to accelerate its beat and blood circulation; this in turn helps to boost body and soul relaxation as well as, the feel of the sense of well-being.

Are there any people out there, who do not wish to possess an excellent health and the feel of well-being? It is humanly natural for every individual to wish and desire to appear and seen as gorgeous, strong and healthy.

Nevertheless, the big question is- how many people in this modern world are able to keep consciously fit through their personal initiatives-without an external assistance?

How many people are able to maintain a sound and stable health for a long time without any form of external assistance other than through constant practice, drive and imagination?

How many people understand, and believe the fact that, everything about their respective health, state of well-being, freedom of all kind and their happiness, solely lie in their hands?

From experience and from the look of things, many people are not aware of these facts and few are very much aware of them, but are reluctant to combine the stress and grind of regular exercises with the present modern lifestyle where most of the works are conducted in closed offices.

Many of the jobs which, we do today are designed to make us sit behind a computer for hours at a stretch, or standing on our feet for hours manipulating machines and other such tasks.

Fact remains that, by the time people leave their respective places of work and get home, these people will surely be subdued by fatigue; mostly out of constant routine than of real tiredness from the work they do or did.

In some cases, some of the people caught in that triangle will try to- make some exercises in order to subdue acquired stress and boredom but will unfortunately discover that their inner spirit is not enthusiastic enough to go along with their body's needs.

"The body is willing but the spirit is very weak" as the saying goes!

- In all, it feels so good to sit your 'butt' in your swivel-chair in front of your Computer (and being served and entertained by Microsoft, goggle, Apple) and other social networks all day working in an office and other such sedentary jobs.

- Sedentary lifestyle does not help your blood circulation and the enhancement of your body muscles; if this continues for a long time, there may be very detrimental effects to the smooth functioning of your body and soul.

For good health and long life, in general, you must always do things that really accelerate your heartbeats even for few minutes daily; flush your blood outlets or veins and your skin pores through body sweat.

Experience shows that nearly all human possess that secret desires to do their very best for themselves; to be the very best that they can be.

Desires to live long and never to die prematurely and have the very best of all material possession possible that they can afford.

Nevertheless, the big question is- at the end of the day, how many people do truly realize and achieve these goals to their satisfaction?

The proliferation of gyms and health spa, hospitals and pharmacies plus places of worship of varying categories are clear demonstrations of that strong inner and secret desires of all people to get better and to have the best out of life. But, unfortunately, from the look of things- the large number of sick and unhealthy people around; the large number of people with problem of obesity, anorexics or bulimia; and the large number of people fanatically and devotedly seeking spiritual salvation through prayers at all cost.

In a nutshell all of the above clearly shows that "many are truly called; but few are truly chosen" as the holy bible says!

The above premise makes 'the wise' to understand that many people do not know about themselves because the true meaning of knowing oneself also goes in context with knowing the kind of food that is good for your stomach to digest better for maximum benefit to your entire system.

Entails also, knowing how to gradually nurse your body, your soul, do your daily work, exercise at the same time and keep a positive mind to achieve that secret desire of having the best and being the best that you would like to be and have. These things are the gift of nature for all to possess, there is no magic to it except that of learning to acquire wisdom and keeping a positive mental attitude which harmonizes the forces of nature to make things work out as though with magical sticks.

The Good News-

The good news is that, whenever anyone learns to understand and control his or her mind's chemistry, his or her eating, playing and working habits tend to improve dramatically. The person will tend to get better in the most natural form; and then transforms toward his or her possible best. Enthusiasm for life and positive things will usually begin to rush back to that person from out of some hidden compartments afterwards.

When you find yourself under such positive mental attitude:

You will begin to feel that you can do those things that seemed impossible before.

Automatically, you will begin to feel that yes, you can do it and do it right.

You will start to train your body and soul following your own natural pace and without the need to rely on a coach; on weight lifting or any other form of external methods or things that are not original from within you.

The above are one of the ways, which nature rewards those people who appreciate themselves and things they already possess. At this stage, you find out that you will begin to cut down and save on doctor's bills; because, you have started to run your things well and you have learnt to be your own coach and your own mentor. These things are simple for those who have faith and confidence in themselves to do. In addition, they will notice gradual and positive changes taking place in their respective lives; as if by magic.

MUSIC AND SOUND

- Dancing and Singing should be Encouraged in every Nation for all Citizens-

Music and harmonious sound is one of the best moral activator very positive for the mind. It ranks high among the greatest gifts of nature duly intended by the Creator to thrill and awaken every kind of human spirit as and when the occasion demands. Above all, music never fails to imbue rich positive vibration wherever music is played; heard of or listened to.

What then is Music?

A dictionary defines music as-"a combination of sounds which express ideas or emotions by the use of rhythm, melody etcetera".

Certainly, everyone possesses the natural instinct to express ideas and emotions. Everyone is capable of humming, whistling, singing or shaking the body in response to emotion. Everyone with or without sight and hearing are, also, capable to read and listen to the ideas or messages delivered through music.

Music is part of human nature and has always been there in different ways from time immemorial.

There are today infinite names of known and unknown musicians from every nook and cranny of the world; so also, there are infinite list of recorded music in the world today through various devices intended to motivate and elevate the soul and the spirit of people, to higher dimensions of rhythmic emotion and spiritual ascension.

However, the thing of interest here is that despite all activities, functions and benefits of music, a large number of people still find it hard to dance, sing or express musical feelings without being shy and restraint. Only few people do it well enough because they take it as a profession and practice dancing and singing; some with mixed feelings of shyness therefore unable to express and show their emotions as they are really feeling it.

Worst still, a good number of people don't express emotions to music. They rather expend their positive energy suppressing than expressing the emotions of music, which they naturally feel deep down-within.

It is a crime against oneself considering the various numbers and categories of recorded music within everyone's reach to see people not in a position to give at least ten- minutes of their time out of twenty-four hours in a day to listen, dance or hum to music.

Everyone needs some dose of music- dancing, singing and laughing on a daily basis. That also, may require only a bit of discipline to attune one's mind to doing so; it's not such a tedious task.

Dancing and singing to any form of music is recommended as a sound-health tonic. It is a very good therapy for the mind, body and soul. It makes you feel like a child each time you are riding with it and in it! Why not keep 'boogieing' with it then.

THE FEMALE HUMAN SPECIE

-More Respect and Leadership Responsibilities to our Female Gender-

In conformity with this new era of doing things differently, the female human species should be given the chance to head most of the political organs of the government in relation to administration and management. While the male specie should assist in all administrative and governmental affairs but, can notwithstanding, be allowed to head and man the rest of the duties that may require more physical energy expenditure.

From the look of things and because, men had always been there from the beginning-imposing, commanding and managing most things of creation, up to this day. Since nothing in life is permanent, we think it will be appropriate also to make a change in the order of things of creation. The change here should begin by reversing that unfair and erroneous notion of male superiority over the female; of women being inferior to their male counterparts; in which factual way are the male more: prominent, superior and more important or productive?

If we knock off pride, prejudice and superstition and honestly compare man and woman in order of selfless services rendered that enriches human life and things; citing examples with instances of pregnancy, family building and positive vibrations surrounding each family atmosphere etc. we will unequivocally conclude that women are no less superior in any way whatsoever to their male counterparts. Rather, the feminine gender is in my view more superior to their male partners surveyed under the umbrella of honesty, and based on services and sacrifices rendered to every society. The women are the real harbinger of good will and progress..., they are the guardians of our racial continuity and perpetuity.

In a normal family set-up; the man wakes up every morning, takes his cutlass or other similar farm tools to work for food for the family existence. But, these days instead, the man drives his vehicle to work for wage and bring money or food home and with that his job for the day, for the family is done in most cases. Meanwhile, the woman is always there from dawn to dusk keenly busy with every family member and house chores; she shoulders as well the inconveniences of nine months pregnancy through to delivery; nursing and feeding each child all through to adulthood; shopping, cooking and caring for all family members through-out her blessed life. Today, our women are increasingly being over burdened with the responsibilities of also bringing food home to top-up their already over scheduled burden with family nurture.

She is in most cases, responsible for the house shores and orderliness. Above all, she manages to support an arrogant and immature-man; showering everyone with love and well wishes with that constant smile on her 'angelic face'; she seems to be always coated with burning desires for: love, peace, harmony and progress!

The female gender usually shows maturity and discipline, which are the basic and rare qualities required for effective leadership dispensation and dissemination!

The female gender in vast majority possesses those cosmic acceptable qualities or positive character trait which nourishes love, unity and peace.

The global community should jointly return or surrender the mantle of leadership to the female gender because; it is their natural and inherent birthright; to guard and guide their children with motherly love for peace's sake. Give this notion a trial at least, considering that men have been in this business of leadership for a long time, welding power and authority yet, our nations and world seem to be negatively progressing instead of positively moving forward on axis with love, unity and affection.

The ex-NIPH students will have to look meticulously into this important notion as to draft out the best possible solution in context to this author's view.

MARRIAGES AND DIVORCES

-No More Divorce after Marriage Vows-

What is Marriage?

'Marriage is an agreement between two opposite sex with a common aim- to live and share things and their life in general; forever and ever, while exploring and exploiting the pleasure in sexual relationship for the main purposes of reproduction and multiplication; for the continuity of humankind.

If the above premise is accepted as being correct therefore, all the ceremonies which we deliberately attach to marriages, are not really necessary. In addition, to this very context, it is obvious that most countries in the world have adopted all sorts of superstitious practices with which to express and consummate this unique natural act of love, sex and reproduction which is solely responsible for the continuity and the regeneration of entire human race!

The religious organizations have specific rules and conditions that have to be observed and followed by all their members or adherents, in order to be legally endorsed as a married couple! – The Roman Catholics, Muslims, Hindus, Tribal and Civil marriages etcetera. All those organs reserve their respective views and opinions regarding marital relationships over moral, social and material conducts for all their true adherents.

From the natural point of view; before a couple decides to go into marital relationship, prior to coming together as one in God and half of each other, they must have been courting for a while in most cases, in and out of bed practicing 'pre-sex' before the final decision to marry. Such acts are natural instincts, therefore normal.

But, the only unfortunate situation is the high rate of divorce and separation we do encounter daily these days, why? What is supposed to be the causes for these rampant divorces especially in the technologically advanced countries of the world?

What is Divorce?

Divorce is disavowing or nullification of the oath of marriage; or the breakup of marriage agreement between two people to live and share their lives together forever.

What then are the main causes of these rampant divorces?

-From the look of things, it is observed that a good number of marriage agreements were usually contracted with many misgivings; due mostly, to the lack of adequate knowledge or experience at the very moment to embark upon that life-changing journey – marriage!

- Most people are not able to determine the extent of the burden and responsibility that living and sharing one's life with someone else could carry. Because, by meeting someone with whom to 'tango', establish an intimate relationship, and possibly go into marriage, had always been a casual and spontaneous affair. There are no mapped-out rules or ways to go about those kinds of things except by personal instincts and casual intents.

-As a result, many chose what you might term as wrong or improper partners thereby leading to short instead of long relationships.

In some areas couple are matched-up together in strict adherence to cultural, traditional or social reasons; while many others meet or link through normal process of courtship before taking the decision to be married to one another.

Nevertheless, unfortunately, in recent years, there is no day that passes without something going wrong somewhere in a matrimonial home of one or two people. It is the news of the day carried out as usual by majority of our News Media outlets: divorces, separations, alimony, mal-treatment and sometimes homicide or physical injuries taking places in some marriage homes etcetera. In fact, the causes of divorces are innumerable because nearly every culture observes what they consider standard moral and social conducts between couples in the gridlock of marriages; and of course, consequently, couples will seek divorce whenever they wish to discontinue or cannot live up to the marriage vows any more.

The Main Causes of Divorces in Marriages Includes-

-Ignorance of nature's intention regarding reproduction and multiplication – you do not have to be married to reproduce and aid in the continuity of humankind in this world; it's your natural gift or assignment as a living being just like the rest of the living creatures, starting from insects to animals.

-Over or under-estimation of oneself- pride, fear and arrogance can cause so much havoc in any family where they are harboured.

-Lack of sense of responsibility- being unable to stand by your spiritual vow is a kind of betrayal whatsoever your reason maybe; you cannot take an oath, a vow to something you cannot maintain even in adversity. It is same as irresponsibility. If you cannot keep your oath of marriage, then don't be in the marriage vow, marriage is not a natural obligation; it is a convenience design of humans. There is no sin against no one if you remain without a marriage partner...better that way than to go in and out of marriages; bear children here and there and without any concrete plans to their growth and sound education; those days are over for good

-Greed, selfishness and avarice – it is naturally difficult to live and share with someone with the above attitude. Without the ability to freely give and share, smooth relationships between two people will be hampered and jeopardized.

-Long hours at work by parents – The social obligation imposed on parents through long working hours does not actually help most to concentrate on their children's moral and family education. It is natural that when a man or woman spend many hours at monotonous and boring daily activities, coming home exhausted; it will be hard to give adequate and sound attention to the affairs of the family.

-Long hours in school by children – It is all right to go to school, but, because the parents have to also spend lengthy hours at work leaving their children's fate in the hands of strangers, who we call teachers. At the end of the day, what happens in between going and coming back from school in most cases neither parents nor teachers could give a valid account of those hours; this move does not help the marriage relationship and build a happy family when the child is out of control.

-Selfishness among some couples - no doubt between two people it will take a lot of understanding to live, work and do all their things with the same spirit of oneness and togetherness. The moment any of these two begin to think more of self, things will surely begin to go wrong and this is one of the major causes of divorces or marital separations.

-Dishonesty and infidelity seem to be the most prominent. Once suspicion and uncertainty sets into the mind of one of the couple, the usual enthusiasm and warmth between both couple will tend to dampen and gradually quarrel will set-in; this is human nature. Those with hot temper will start breaking plates, tearing photos and destroying things which, once were of value to both of them.

-What about a violent and jealous husband or wife who derives undue pleasure quarrelling, hurting and destroying each other?

The lists of things that can go wrong in marriages are too many to account for in a short book of this nature. Irrespective of our human perception of the so-called marriage relations, what then is the appropriate way to go about marriages and marriage relationship? Is it naturally necessary to be married in the first place for the world of human race to continue to multiply and go ahead with their lives here on Mother Earth? Your intimate answers are required, please.

NATURE'S INTENTION FOR MARRIAGE

In marriage, the final aim or the natural intention for a man and a woman to agree to live together is none other than to explore and enjoy each other's sex organs, share everything and assist each other to build a family full of children and hope; that is one of the human intentions for going into marriages; but also, to fulfil nature's project for reproduction and multiplication of human race; to aid the smooth continuity of humankind as it is for the rest of the living and non-living things of creation.

However, nowadays, those main motives do not seem to be the issue any more in the highly competitive marriage arena. Most couples do not put that, the main motive for marrying into primary consideration when time to tango. Instead, wedding rings, wedding-dresses, roses, personal interest, and material aggrandizement coupled with grand and ostentatious marriage ceremonies largely overshadow each couple's mind from start.

As a result, marriage is no more for love-sake; and to build a united, disciplined and culturally enriched family, which is supposed to continue to replicate and maintain human populace of their kinds. That gross act of omission or commission by humankind is making a big mess of this fundamental act of marriage. Most marital homes are regularly being broken with their devastating effects over nature's sense of harmony. There are many human factors responsible for these marriage failures.

Major Reasons Most Marriages Fail to Stabilize and Endure-

- Most people go into marital relationship, instead of concentrating both of their efforts on building loved and sound children to aid the prosperity of their family; they rather concentrate their positive energy on building wealth and fame at the expense of Nature's intention for marriages or smooth human relationships!

- Most go into marital relationship, instead of concentrating both of their efforts on learning to understand themselves better, share ideas, plan and work together towards a common goal for both of them, and for the family in general but, instead they take opposite stance.

- Our justified and accepted social obligations rather tend to put most marriages asunder rather than binding them together.

- Today, every parent spends hours at a monotonous job away from home; their children on the other hand spending most of their precious time at boring schools in the hands and care of strangers as teachers. Some leave their beloved children in the cares of house carers and friends.

But then, we all agree that "charity should begin at home" in which way could you truly impart and impact on your children so that they will grow up embodying your moral impetus, if you were never there to educate them with what you know; or give to them whatever you have got, talent wise and other-wise?

-The questions are – does doing things in these ways truly represent those charitable homes worthy of emulation, which we fight and aim to achieve?

-Do those ways fulfil and comply with the natural or divine intentions and purposes of raising rich happy families? Answers are no.

As in many other aspects of life, the value of marriages and rearing families is being wrongly misinterpreted, due mostly to the same ignorance of the creator's intentions for man and woman to tango or due to outright disobedience of cosmic laws universally ruling over things of creation.

It is because of all these wrong interpretations, reasons and values of marriage that rampant cases of divorce, alimony, separation, single mothers/fathers, have become a household vocabulary. Indirectly also, for these reasons - abortion, abandoned children, depression, loneliness, prostitution, infidelity, betrayals are on the increase; for the same reason also, the direct fruits or offspring from the umbrella of such unstable families produces: disobedient, angry and undisciplined children who shall be emerging and emanating like locust out of such kinds of marital homes.

Are these the kind of family we vowed and promised to uphold until death when we take the oath of allegiance in or for marriage?

How do you think you can make or raise rich, healthy, happy and loving children with those inherited or acquired problems?

My view is that it will be impossible if we fail to see marriages as man-made obligations and to place love as a prime factor before making children. You have no obligations to marry for children! "If you can't pay the time, don't commit the crime" "If you can't be there to teach and educate your children yourself, don't produce babies"

TRANSPORTATION AND AUTOMOBILE

-Free National Transportation Services for all Citizens-

Is there any reason why we cannot permit 'free transportation services for all citizens of this nation or of this world if can put greed and pride aside just for a moment?

Without an iota of doubt, the very invention and advent of automobiles is among others, one of the most important technological achievements by human race. We are all aware of and conversant with the numerous kinds of transportation mechanisms in this wide world, ranging from: Bicycles, Motor Cycles, Tricycles- (like the Indian Rickshaw), Quads, Auto-Cars, Buses, Trains, and Airplanes to Ships etc. Any of the above transport medium will 'jolly-ride you around; some across oceans and clouds; permit me to use this medium to thank and congratulate the inventors and manufacturers of all those transport systems which have in so many ways, improved humans and all forms of life; as well as, their living conditions for centuries. All human lives have improved extraordinarily in recent times due mostly to the availability of automobiles without doubt.

Did humans not survive those eras, when there was no transportation system? Certainly, all humans are made to survive under any kind of condition or situation. Humans are malleable and flexible. They can adapt to varying conditions of life; as we are for example, now- living in the era of pure stress and struggle for nearly all things, whether it is 'man-made' or 'nature-made'.

In the olden days when there were no vehicle-transportations, we could walk for days covering distances and getting most things done well and better even.

However, we should recognize how tedious and tiring walking for long could be (nevertheless, walking is recommended for the good it does to your dear health).

For the love of peace and harmony in this new order of things, **I hereby suggest and endorse free transportation systems for all humans;** and with the following cogent reasons:

-Vehicles were invented to aid and assist people to move from one point to the other; with goods and objects of varying dimensions in bid to relief the former strain of walking on foot for hours and days to a given destination. In addition, to relief the burden upon the beasts that were usually transporting heavy loads for us in the recent past, such as donkeys, horses etc.

-Use of vehicle is making it possible for families to live far away from each other and still commune regularly whenever and wherever they want.

-Use of vehicle have helped humans a lot in reaching and developing rural areas which otherwise, will be unreachable by any other means. In fact, without the invention and use of vehicles and other machineries, human history today would have being different. Obviously, vehicle usage has become next to nature for humanity.

Vehicle Inconveniences-

Unfortunately, the obvious jolly-ride, which vehicles were supposed to offer to humans, is now becoming a serious nightmare.

-Vehicle prices are so irrationally exorbitant that billions of world citizens are unable to own or use any.

-Vehicle ride is so dangerous that millions of humans die regularly on our roads; even as I am writing and as you are reading, someone is dying somewhere around the world right now from vehicle related accidents.

-Vehicle usage dramatically increased every level of imaginable crimes ranging from: wars, kidnapping, car bombing, drug trafficking, sexual abuse and human trafficking. The list of negative and positive activities the use of vehicles has enhanced are innumerable.

-Vehicle stress related situations are too many to mention, beginning from their complicated manufacturing processes to registration, licensing to the constant pollution it carries along.

-Then come down to the vehicle owner who is obliged to go to driving school, learn synchronized driving styles, road and sign-boards; registration of vehicle on their names, pay exorbitant prices which they usually spend all their life paying without end.

-Vehicle Insurance, "who really invented that 'leech' or blood-sucking vampire"? It is one of the most annoying forms of organized crime with open intimidation! Why not accept certain amount of money on a given vehicle and that will be it; instead of making people pay through all their lives just to own a deadly vehicle? Why do you love money more than you do love people? It is a shame on humanity and disappointing to the Creator of all things. Know that nothing really belongs to us; for everything we have is borrowed; for this fact, I suggest that-**Vehicle use should be free for all human races!**

How Can We Scheme a Free Transportation for all Humans?

-The ex-NIPH students will setup **'National Headquarters for all Vehicle-Brands'** that will have to legally approve or permit the manufacture of any vehicle-brand designed by any manufacturer from any part of the world.

-Vehicles being such a fast and vast mortal weapon despite their best services to humanity, before any of their manufacture or production- design, security and safety standards from the **National Headquarters for all Vehicle-Branding'** must be met by vehicle manufacturers through certified approval from the NHVB.

- All vehicles, whether small or big, must be incorporated with 4wheel-drive for easier and safer access on all terrains.

- We should henceforth stop the manufacture of small cars; fortify the strength and security levels of those approved for production and public use.

-One vehicle only, will be permitted for every couple and their children; single people have no need for a private vehicle.

-All public transportation networks should be from the global headquarters; and distributed to the remotest part of this earth. Even car-rental businesses will be handled by the NHVB. (The modus operandi shall be discussed later on a board meeting)

-Vehicle manufacturers must sell their manufactured vehicles directly to the NHVB under an agreement; they will in turn make the vehicle sale and distribution to the public under a generally accepted procedure.

-Every region or city must have their central representatives who will be solely dependent on the directives of NHVB in charge of making transportation available at all time of the clock for the services and needs of the people of that said region.

To What Advantages are These Transport Regulations in this new Order of Things?

-To reduce to the barest minimum, the number of people dying daily all over the world, caused by vehicle accidents of varying degrees.

-To reduce the psychological stress caused by such factors as: buying, owning and maintaining a vehicle; most people are forced to buy a vehicle because of work-demands – maybe where you live is not easily accessible to public transport-stations; time of work-fixtures and all such situations. -Most people own a vehicle only to show-off and please their ego-demands.

-However, whatever your reasons to own a car, such reasons cannot compensate for the pollutants emitted, from the vehicles you use. The city congestion; the accidents and the noises… we will make sure that people should with ease, go wherever they want and whenever they want, through adequate provision of prompt services in order to encourage people, to sacrifice for the new system of things to function better for the benefit of all citizens…!

BUSINESSES AND NORMS

-More Time for Family and Nature; Reduced Business or Work Hours -

What is Business?

Business is simply: the act of doing anything whatsoever for economic rewards.

From the past human history and to these present global political dispensations, it's obvious that majority of human race spend almost all their precious time in pursuit of economic rewards and material gains at the very expense of the true human values and realities.

Why Do They Do That?

Is that the best way you have to make you feel good and at peace?

How could you give away for so little as 'money', most of your precious and invaluable time that is naturally given to you to do things for yourself and for those around you, especially between you and your very direct family?

How can you neglect yourself by not making out time for the humane activities as: reasoning in silence between yourself and your Creator, meditating in the open air and with clear mind, give time to study about yourself and try to know the real you and what you really want out of this conglomerate and infinite abundance of creation?

With a bit of wisdom and deeper knowledge for sound living, you will perceive the futility of taking yourselves too serious while in normal pursuit of your dreams and aspirations in this very life that we are living. You should rather strive to pursue your goals and aspirations with high enthusiasm, humility and joy from the challenges they usually offer. Knowing that, whatever you may invent or create today or tomorrow to come in this very world, will only serve to bring, *'just momentary joy and aggrandizement with material achievement'*.

Everything whatsoever with their respective rules for people and other creatures had long been stipulated, structured and concluded with, through the miracle of the Creator!

Your main purpose in life is nothing more than making good use of all that nature has stockpiled for your entertainment; while you grow with them and ultimately die and rot away within the structured rules of general life'.

When you grow enough to perceive your life's purpose and those of others, you will then surely know that the only realistic joy that you can rightly derive out of all the elements of life is: *the act of sharing and giving; sharing unconditionally with enthusiasm everything you have gotten from ideas, jokes to material things. Such attitude to life adds enormous benefits to your body, mind and soul.*

Know also that, obsessive accumulation of material things by a nation or person is a sign of ignorance and of course, pride and the fear of lack. More things you have, more problems of stress you will equally accumulate in proportion to your acquired material possession and which will ultimately compound your harmonious existence at long. Therefore, you should do away with most things that are inimical to the peace and happiness of your soul.

Make more effort to select businesses that give you joy instead of stress and sleeplessness.

This being so, it is therefore stupid to spend your precious time in vain pursuit of money and material aggrandizement at the very expense of your peace and harmony. Henceforth, we should spend more time and make most effort to build rich, healthy and happy families. We should take our lives more seriously; given that our respective lives are more precious than Gold and Silver or any other thing in planet earth whatsoever.

Question is: **will it be better for you to have all the wealth in this world at the expense of your unique health and life?**

My own answer is absolute NO! Send your own answers and comment to this question please.

Without health, your money and businesses are useless to you of course. So, why all these craze, betrayals and anxiety for money and businesses; what sense is there in all that upheaval at the expense of family and self?

Think my people; think deeper and reason!

As the national and global community gets wiser, this world will get better and every creational thing and humans will begin to change to their best ever. You will discover then, to your dismay, that all your accumulated wealth had been wasted labor. Because, with a Positive Mental Attitude to life, wealth and material aggrandizement take the lowest place of significance in the scale of 'life's values' and this can happen easily in this new era of things. Thanks to this new national and global easy access to information for all citizens. For that, collectively, we owe unreserved gratitude to those behind the Information Technology and Media-Networking projects!

HOUSING AND LAND MANAGEMENT

-Lands and Houses should be Free for all Citizens-

-People should stop buying or selling of either lands or houses. Lands do not belong to anyone; lands are the exclusive property of the Creator. Just like seas, stars, moon, sun, sky, the cloud and the air we breathe; those are exclusive reserves of nature for all at no cost.

- Land is just one of those elements of nature created for our collective succor and nurture; land is not a thing to own, it is not a belonging; unbelievable that we, the global citizens had continued from time immemorial to encourage that wrongdoing of buying and selling lands which is an exclusive property of the Creator!

-Humanity should not own lands outside of the land in which you live and work on.

-It is really ugly and repulsive for humans to engage in such negative actions; no doubt, if you could find a way to do it, you will be buying and selling the air that we breathe, the sea that flows, the stars and moon that shines and the sun that warms and lights all things!

Why is this over anxiety for money and material possession taking hold of the entire global community? I am ashamed most times for being part of human species due to their negative attitude and gross sign of ingratitude to the Creator of this world and its creatures. Sorry, you need to forgive my outbursts, just can't hold it sometime when contemplating the outstanding level of devastation and the gross aloofness over steps for mitigating possible future damages...

Guidelines for Uniform Dispensation of Available Lands and Properties

Once a boy and a girl come of age and decide to marry each other, as a couple, they will be given a pre-mapped piece of land in any chosen community where said couple will want to live, so that they can cultivate, grow their own food, raise their children and multiply without anyone on their shoulders.

-Shelter or a house is the number two most important of the three basic needs of human beings, after food. It therefore beats my imagination why humans, are not able to freely utilize the vast lands naturally given to them for their collective use and for sustenance on earth while they grow, multiply, then die and rot away; instead of one person, State or organization accumulating and hoarding lands and properties meant for all citizens to share and enjoy?

-If all the other creatures: animals, insects, fishes micro and macro-organisms live freely in and on the lands, seas, jungles, air etc, why then must human race be made to pay to own a piece of land to shelter them in order to sustain their existence on Mother-Earth? Does that make any sense to you? Think about it! Why must we pay for everything from the day we were born to the day we die; what then are our collective spiritual and material inheritances from our overall Creator; what is our collective essence of lives here on earth?

-Something is obviously wrong with humans, for accepting and thriving or struggling in such kinds of chaotic ventures- scrambling and shamelessly scampering for lands you did not own or create?

- Every family has a birth-right to a piece of land and the natural obligation to produce at least one regular eatable item as one´s own contribution to Mother-Nature and our perpetuity.

- Every human must be given the chance and appropriate coaching on how to produce most of the things that they consume on daily basis such as: rearing animals, planting fruit trees, vegetables or cultivate tubers etc. for it will be a shame and utterly against Mother-Nature for any human to go through life without producing at least one eatable item; such negative trend is inimical to the progress and prosperity of this nation and world at large. Such conducts and approach to life is the same thing as being a parasite; an unwanted weed in someone's vegetable farm! Get up, get lands and cultivate your own food stuffs; do it for yourself and for our Creator.

- Having all the money and properties in this world without producing most or any of the food you eat daily, you are not setting a good example to the youths in this way. Can you directly eat your money or property? Answer is no! You need food to live in a house. Therefore, you should have known to produce some of the food you and your family eat everyday to help in nature building. 'I very well understand the past and present global economic trends; the concept in favor of the popular phrase "Division of Labor" and its connotations; so far so good for only the unseen perpetrators of the human rules and regulations.

However, the big question remains- 'Is this current ways we run our societies the best approach on how to live with nature, ourselves and achieve balanced progress and prosperity?

To this fundamental topic, the ex-NIPH students will find a way to harmonize such issues as land and housing and management in a way to enhance equity and fairness.

Land and houses must be free for all national or global citizens and every global citizen on their own should produce at least one edible item wherever they live; whether in the desert, snow, forest, city and villages! In this new era there will be no excuse whatsoever for any human not to have a place to live nor something to cultivate with money or no money.

If we want, yes we can! This time around, we all really should want it for peace and harmony to reign supreme everywhere! On my own, I am utterly sick of the ways we run our shits here on earth. I know we can do even eighty-times-more-than all we have ever done, if we all agree to agree-in all these efforts, I only want to see nations in love, in peace, unity and harmony with everything and every human, plants and animals…life will be good for all for it don´t you think so?

SPORTS-ARTS-AND-CULTURE

-All Human must Practice any form of Arts or daily Sports-

Why must people practice sports, arts or culture? Does it matter to anyone what people do or not with their self?

-Truth is, human beings like most other creatures are structured to undergo through regular body, mind and soul maintenance with the work and exercise they do, in order to remain fit, happy and healthy.

-Yes it matters to me what you choose or will choose to do with yourself; why? Because to realistically live a successful and "good life", you need to have or store enough energy reserve. Yes, you need a lot of energy even to be happy, dance and laugh deeply; to play well, you will need positive energy to do everything well. Putting that into perspective, you will agree with me that it is absolute nonsense for anyone to live without sports, arts and cultural practices; particularly for the good benefits we derive out of doing them…

The ideal and natural food for your mind is the intangibles such as: imagination, all physical and mental activities; as well as regular adventure which provides experiences that in turn balances the physical brain-chip. While the physical food that we consume help to align our entire body cells which in turn sustains the energy force or engine of life.

In this new order of things, we want to see majority of human beings more healthy, happy and prosperous. When you are healthy, you can be happier and enjoy life with more enthusiasm than when you are ill at ease sick.

Do not wait for doctors, start practicing any activity of your choice that you can do on regular basis; prevention is always better than cure; do you not agree any more to that old adage?

Do not wait to be sick before you can take your health seriously. Take care of yourself with all your energy; with every single thing at your disposals. Life has no duplicate!

By the way, is there any other thing in your life that is more important than you yourself are? Answer is no! If you know that you are the most important thing in your life, why then neglect your good self as you presently do?

Activities or any form of physical and mental exercise help in no small measures to fortify your brain-chip, your physical body and all the body organs that sustain the smooth functioning of your entire being. So go for it now for your own good and that of national and global peace and harmony! When you are healthy and happy, every other thing and people around you will as well, in equal proportion, be healthy and happy! This is how we want our world citizens to be and to feel in this new era of our lifetime…

CHILDREN AND THE FUTURE

-Today's Children will definitely become Tomorrow's Parents and Leaders-

-If you agree with me that, the children of today will definitely become parents and future leaders, why then do we disrespect our beloved children and treat their matters without much consideration or as second-class citizens, or as people whose values are set far in future; when they grow after the age of eighteen?...

For example, we have coined and retained in our global lexicon such phrases as "You are acting like a child" "you are just a child" what are the literal meanings of such expressions?

Literally, such expressions or phrases could mean that the 'child' or children is/are stupid; nonchalant, or utterly unreliable and non-dependable. The expression could also mean that, the 'child' is irresponsible and does not know how to act appropriately.

All over the world, there are laws based on the ages of children; for example, the age from which the children have to start and finish schooling; from what age they could be allowed to participate in certain sports activities; and at what age to drive, smoke or drink…the list of things children cannot do or participate in with their parents or on social levels are innumerable.

- Until eighteen years of age in most European countries, you are considered a child without right to do most things you see your parents do daily; such as: drinking of alcoholic contents, smoking cigarettes, marijuana or any intoxicant. Even driving or travelling on their own, without permissions is not permitted till the leaders decide.

-In some countries they peg the age at sixteen before a growing child is considered an adult and with rights to do things they desire. And in some other places, children have no written age limits as in most Africa or parts of Asia, in such places, for a child to be considered an adult with rights of decision and participation in what presumed adults are doing; the parents or cultural backings determine when their growing children should be duly accepted as grown-up adults! Whatever the reasons, the criteria or motives for such laws and attitude toward our beloved children, I have no idea; all I do know is that we claim and assume that, we are trying to do our best for our beloved children; bla-bla-bla...

-I only want to use this medium to bring it to your knowledge, that, the approach to the education of our children– world future leaders- is not the right way to go about it. It is not appropriate to discriminate against our children, oblige them always not to do things off their own volition; for instance schooling, driving, and use of many things they are not allowed while their parents do and use those things. That is share hypocrisy and senseless approach!

-Bear in mind when a given child receives the appropriate and sound education from earlier age, that child can do so many things much more responsibly than even the adults do.

-I have seen, known and lived with children who are much cleverer than their parents are; do their things and manage their lives much better than their parents do.

- If we educate our children with the correct stuff in their mind, they will surely behave well; which means they can do whatever adults are doing if we allow and encourage them.

-I feel it is more correct that we should let our children begin early enough to experience and discover about life through their personal trials and errors or out of their experiences.

To protect children from danger is to deny them of the ability to develop their own natural survival instinct and discourage them also, from life of adventure; that should not be the correct thing to do, or the 'proper way to position them for life ahead'.

I have written a book based on these issues with the title –"How to Educate Children with Ease"- see book at http://www.amazon.com/author/amaechiobi

- I noticed that children begin to use their minds almost as fully as their parents do, from the age of five years upwards. At this age, they can do whatever the adults are doing. In fact, our children generally prefer to do whatever we, their parents are doing; they like to and feel they can if allowed. So let us give our beloved children that benefit to make mistakes and learn from their respective mistakes; to be in danger and learn to fight their respective ways out of said dangers.

Why should our children be eighteen or be given any age-peg or limit for them to begin doing things that they can do well today and now if allowed; or all the bureaucratic red tapes removed for them to listen and follow their heart desires without such interferences as listed above?

What Is Therefore The Best Option For Our Children?

-More Respect and Attention to Our Children-

Do you know that every child is born with their own brain-chip in which is deeply engraved the child's unique characteristics concerning their personality trait?

I believe that a child's personality trait is uniquely transferred through the phenomenon- 'DNA'. And I also suspect that DNA molecular contents do continue to shuffle and reshuffle its data; influenced by time factors, geographical position of the parent at the time of a Childs formation; and probably, influenced by the earth position at the precise moment of a child's formation or conception as it revolves around the sun or wherever.

Those natural influences or phenomena may usually determine the personality trait of a given person; and also, may rightly answer the question: why our finger prints varies; why every single human have got a unique finger print and as well, why genealogy can be traced through the DNA-match

Based on the above observations, the ex-NIPH students will have to review the laws governing our future children as to modify certain conditions or influences whether social or within the family, which will psychological and physically favor them, favor their parents, and our collective national and global community without exception.

If today's children will become tomorrow's parents and leaders, it is therefore wise to invest most of our positive energy and wisdom to make them be and have the best of everything possible that we can offer, with love and affection and without any form of reservation.

From the subtle ways of nature and creation which bases on the immutable laws of: "give and take"; "seek and find"; and "do unto others as you would like them to do unto you".

For example, I am rather constrained to suggest that, we should revise and modify the present national and global work-schedule. Scheme positive plans in

such a way as to give enough time to every family; to take care of them, especially, care for their children. Because, our families form the foundation for the continuity of this world; they reproduce the tomorrow's leaders; and, to give adequate time to our families will be a very important long-term investment that will be benefit all and sundry.

The serious business of running a family should be promoted; be publicized and given as much attention as necessary.

This will surely enhance deep affection for owning and running a family and as well guarantee mature and disciplined children who will be much better than we have them today.

Today's children will automatically become tomorrow's parents and eventual leaders! With this in mind, it will be quite imprudent not to give as much time as possible to families in order to make the best of their children.

I will suggest that we give half of our total daily hours to our children thereby gradually fortifying that fundamental sector of our national and thus; global future investment. Because, *the more time you spend with your children, the more you are bound to know what kind of stuff or traits they are composed of; their natural abilities and inclination and most important also, you will be able to directly impact and impart to them whatever you have to offer as a parent, outside their teachers and external mentors.*

Doing that will give the entire world a better chance to raise children with balanced mental attitude which is most necessary for any kind of human success and progress.

As best option for our children's sake I am suggesting that we try to adopt a policy where each family should not give more than ten working hours daily to public work or services (between wife and husband). The woman will work for five hours and so will the man; or that the man of each family should serve an hour more than the woman if the need be. This suggestion is because the children usually require the attention of both parents for them to have a balanced mental attitude; even both husband and wife will require the steady attention of each other to be in a state of balanced and positive mental attitude to make the responsibility of rearing their given children to blossom.

This kind of project can be enhanced through a system in which we can organize national and global- **Best Family Contest Awards-** this is to encourage families to continue doing their best in bringing up their children. We can also organize other national and States awards for **'The Best Behaved Child/Children'** as well as **The Best Parents of the Year Awards'** etcetera. This will encourage parents to give their best to their children and vice versa.

It is our collective national as well as global duty to make our people understand and to be conscious of the fact that this child-rearing business happens to be the most important aspect of our future lives and should be duly accepted and honored accordingly.

The children and family are globally more beneficial than those of movies and moneymaking are.

We should try to divide the working hours and schedules into four shifts of five hours work with one hour of break for each shift. This also will have the advantage of allowing more families to have jobs to do as well; instead of one

person doing nearly ten hours and above; straight at a given job while others have nothing to do. Also, working for so long at a given job is detrimental to family relationship, friendship and even to personal health.

Doing these will also help to bring back and promote most of the lost values which goes with family relationship in general and which will help to minimize the misconduct of children and the disruption of families that took a lot of pain and hard work to build. This kind of project and plan will surely have huge positive impact on a national and global dimension, and will benefit all of us in the end. These are many of the steps to take if we want to have love, peace, unity and harmony in these awesome nations!

ENOUGH OF NEGATIVITY; EMBRACE POSITIVITY

Stop these "much ado about nothing"; desist from warring and killing each other in the guise of making the world a better place! What is the problem with this world? This world has no problem; you have the problem. Few people in essence are busy creating most of the problems in this world. Can you desist from these frenetic and pathetic races for fame, demonstration of power, competition, and accumulation of material wealth and hoarding of things of creation? "Live and let live"; "do onto others as you would like them to do unto you". This is few of the impeccable rules of the game of life and living; any addition or subtraction is an adulteration, an offence severely punishable under the constitution of 'Creation'. Now is the ripe time for national and global peace, unity in harmony! Our world is full of negative thoughts and intents. Our only savior is to acquire and possess more wisdom; sending good and positive thoughts out to the Universe. That should be our collective salvation from this imminent devastation jarring us face-to-face.

COMPARING FIFTY YEARS BACK DOWN TO THIS DAY:

1. As a child from the early-sixties, I remember walking naked around our house and our neighborhood without feeling shy or any form of quilt. Today, such natural feeling of innocence had been replaced with the ugly feeling of quilt and shyness under the same circumstance; why and what went wrong?

2. I remember also how, we used to swim naked both sexes of our communities: mothers and sons, fathers and daughters, all swimming and playing in the same river without shyness, quilt or any form of negative sentiments. Today, boys and girls of any age are not allowed to associate in any way possible for intimate interactions; what had gone wrong and when did that rupture took place?

3. I also remember as recent as the eighties, how we used to feel deep affection and sympathy for any of our family members to even neighbors when they are in pain from sickness or anything whatsoever abnormal. Today, we instead feel joy and apathetic if our family member or neighbor suffers and in pain; which, in most cases, in these days, we even do things with the intention to bring direct pain and hardship to our own relatives.

4. As a child, I vividly remember how we used to constantly think of what to give, do for or help our direct family and community at adulthood. And, as soon as we reach adult and able, our first income or material gains goes to our beloved parents or brothers and sisters before we shall ever have the sense to think of doing anything for our own personal benefits. Today, hardly do I see or notice such virtue in anyway anywhere whatsoever. What happened? In place of such good deeds, most that I see are children who abuse and insult their parents up to even when they become adults; some accuse their parents of not doing one thing or the other for them; and no matter how much the parents had labored to cater for them. If at adult in these days, a person is unsuccessful, there are always the parents' and the country to blame for his or her plight! Wow! What a great generation of humans we are reproducing and educating? How shall we as people retrieve and revive our extinguishing intrinsic values?

"FROM THEIR FRUITS WE SHALL KNOW THEM"

What Kind of Seeds Have We Sown For Our Nations?

The seeds of division in the place of unity, the seeds of hatred in the place of love, the seeds of destruction in the place of collaboration and the seeds of fear in the place of courage and adventure.

What Kind of Fruits Are We Eating From the Seeds Sown for Us by Our Ancestors?

Obviously, our ancestral seeds have grown to a giant tree producing more: fear, depression, negative stress, hunger, intimidation, diseases and insecurity. On the other hand, our trusted political systems all over the world are dutifully nourishing from those seeds of penury planted through orchestrated wars, assassination, terrorism and propaganda. While most of the media-outlets, schools, churches, associations and cultural heritages dutifully serve in our collective Mind-Control. These are our fruits; the fruits of our inheritance.

From What Sources Do We Acquire the Fruits That Mold and Modify Our Lives?

Through 'THOUGHT or THINKING'- Thought is the source of every seen and unseen thing in this world. Thought is the only possible direct link between humanity and their Divine Energy Source. Knowingly or unknowingly, we have sown the seeds of mediocrity, fear, competition and aloofness through our Negative Leadership Thought Pattern.

To counter these looming problems pervading us on national and global perspectives, our only Divine Remedies or Antidotes are to reshuffle, redesign and restructure our political system of leadership. We can achieve that by planting the good seeds of unity, love, peace and harmony through a "Conscionable-Positive Leadership- Thought

Pattern, nourished and fostered by the deeds of: sharing, giving, serving others, sincerity, openness and by doing more than is required of us at every point ; going the extra-mile. This is our only remedy to plant and harvest the seed of unity, peace and love to all our people and of course, to the wide-wild-World.

Victimization of Biafrans - *In Nigeria & Diaspora*

As an innocent Third World Youth´, born and bred in Biafra – One of the richest and most fertile lands in Africa. I had the fortune or misfortune to witness the long Nigeria/Biafra civil-war which lasted for nearly three-long-years; ending on 15th January 1970 and with a special slogan "NO VICTOR; NO VANQUISHED"; meaning that no side won nor lost- it was just a civil quarrel between brothers and sisters! Amazing people!

I was barely five-years-old when the civil war started in 1967. Needless to describe the horrors of that war because I did not retain a vivid account of things that happened and why they happened except, the little I witnessed which I could remember as a child; read from books as a teenager and from the little that we were told by few historians in abroad who made some effort to write the little or much they knew about the war. This is indeed irrelevant to this book but, just to help you have an idea of some of the past events that jointly molded the Nigeria society as we have it today.

Nigeria in Economic-Boom

One year or two after that 'holistic-war" Nigeria was proclaimed to be in economic-boom by the international community! It was discovered that the country is rich and replete with petroleum and other natural resources. The government and their purported good foreign allies started the construction and re-construction of a devastated nation. Nigerian citizens during that era of economic boom were awarded national free education for all to go to school at all levels! The whole world opened their boarders visa-free for Nigerians to come in and out of their respective countries to spend their oil money; every family were sending their teenagers to Europe and America to attend schools to any level; our parents were busy flying in and out of every country of the world at will, for shopping and vacations. They were very busy spending our oil money and living in an enviable ostentation without obvious goals for the future ahead.

Our good foreign allies were busy siphoning our petroleum money and resources back to their countries- thanks to technological know-how: Texaco, Shell, BP, Chevron and many others. On the other side, the multinational companies as Leventis Stores, Kingsway Stores, Chanrais, UTC, and many others. Fashion sectors you have: Levi, Marks & Spencer, Adidas, Bata, and countless others in every sector of business; from the banking industry: Union bank and their counterparts, it was simply awesome for me as a child to witness those economic development and investment by foreign allies!

The entire nation were in festive mood: our parents were busy importing chains of cars, slaughtering truck loads of Rams and Cows even when they found no good reason to celebrate, they just celebrate anyway to show-off their wealth and to entertain lavishly. They usually spread money on people in any given occasion; wore flamboyant/excessive local made dresses and chieftaincy beads and jewelries; with nearly every family having two to three maids and chauffeurs. Their children have their separate drivers who are always at their whim; taking them to schools and outings etc.

As a kid, I somehow knew that those were not the right ways to a progressive and decent life. Subconsciously, I was constantly irritated, wept all nights instead of having a sound sleep for all the nearer and distant injustices I felt and still feel all around me. For a slight mistake those self proclaimed Bosses will kick the shit out of their drivers and their maids; call them very ugly names which their mouth could utter; punish them in whichever way they deem fit and dishing out curses abundantly without any form of reservation. (Even their colonial masters never treated them as bad!) And as a kid all such actions were ceaselessly hurting my innocent soul. Though, I was fortunate or unfortunate to strongly belong to those privileged class in the entire nation.

All of the above were of course the privileges of the few, while the peasants and the major part of the population were left in the villages to attend to the farms and ancestral houses without: portable waters, electricity, market stalls to sell their farm proceeds; no tarred or un-tarred roads for easy access to and from anywhere. Hospitals were too many luxuries, so is a decent means of transportation for the emerging communities. The only tangible things the poor and majority of the Nigerian masses had till today for all that boom were uncompleted budgets and haphazardly completed ones which usually must crumble within few years of inauguration. Above all that, the then Nigerian currency – NAIRA- was valued above the dollars and the rest of the world currencies except the Pounds. However, for the same colonial reasons and the world political in-balances, the Nigerian Naira was still not accepted anywhere in the world; only currencies as Pounds Sterling and Dollars were!

Anyway, the crux is that that whole bravado lasted for barely fifteen years when in 1986/87 the colonial masters named- International Monetary Fund (IMF) hit the Nigerians below the belt and knocked them off the arena of strong economic nations by devaluing their currency- Naira- and also clamping a huge dept on their head to weaken their growing tails and sprouting wings...this is not relevant also to this book; cited here just to explain why I am a political victim of our world political jamboree; and thank God that my decision, actions ordeal were 'self imposed'; because I wanted to put myself in the shoes of the victimized majorities of our world. And because, I voluntarily refused to accept to belong among the "self-proclaimed-privileged-few" in which, I was rightly born into, I rather chose to feel the pains of the ruled masses and peasants in first-person-experience.

For the above personal reasons best known to me and for my deep pursuit of justice for all humankind, I refused to renounce my nationality even though, I have got the right as I write this piece to ask for and be given: a Dutch nationality, a Spanish nationality and above all an Italian nationality for the fact that, I am happily married to an Italian citizen and with six children to raise. Two of those children were born in Spain where I lived and worked. One was born in Netherlands where I lived and worked. And Italian because by right of marriage, I could ask and be granted Italian citizenship after six months of marriage but, I am over fifteen years in marriage, presently live and work in Italy against my volition but voluntarily refused to renounce my Nigerian nationality for Italian or for any other; but, however great my decisions and actions may sound, they have their enormous sacrifices which are all to my own detriment. *My big question being-* **"must everyone have to be converted to European and American citizens in order to become a cogent human-being or bona-fide global citizen?**

Your answers and opinions are required from everyone who cares about this rupture in our present worldly situation!

In a way, I somehow feel trapped in this mesh of global incongruence: I do not want to live here; do not want to live in any part of the first world countries and yet, can't just pack and go home to my beloved third world Nation because my ancestral home had continuously been eroded, sabotaged by our national and international leaders (Twice I went home with my entire family; another long story on its own) where all my human rights and dignity should remain ever-intact; but, due to organized political betrayals and human manipulations between the "Third World" political incumbents in ally with their "First World political" sharks, who are ready to sink the entire world and devour anyone that makes the least attempt to question or oppose their selfish laws and regulations!

- I am not saying that everything about first and second worlds is evil and negative, no. All I am saying is that, if we collectively agree with each other in an honest and sincere spirit, we can no doubt do much more than we are doing or have ever done for the benefit of the entire universe! Not just you or me but for us; that is the positive way to reason, that is the way I would like our fathers who are our leaders to think, reason and enact the laws that bind and guide us all as one in a family. No other way I can see: peace, unity and harmony achieved for the benefit of all!-

 I could not take my lovely children back to my Third World nation for all such uncertainties taking place everywhere that I went; having lived and worked half of my life in the First-World for this long. Sometime in 2002, enraged with anger for many good reasons, I took my entire family from Netherlands back to the Gambia to settle and live the rest of my earth life over there, with my children and beloved wife. My wife at then was laden with children of varying age differences; she was seven-month-pregnant at the time with another eleven-month-old baby still breastfeeding, five-year-old, seven-year-old, thirteen-year-old and fifteen-year-old children. To make that trip, I left behind me everything I owned and worked for. My anger was too deep that if I didn't leave, I might do something outrageous and probably end up in jail for a long time! Similar thing happened when I was in the Canary Island of Spain, I was also forced to abandon my house and all my properties because of this my inability and weakness to stomach any form of injustice – I know I could kill with pleasure for the sake of justice, but my deepest love for humans make me incapable not even to employ the use of harsh words to hurt people's feelings; I will rather suffer and nurse my pains alone than to inflict pains to others. "Nonsense!" but that is me and my story; no regrets of any kind whatsoever.

Two months in the Gambia my wife delivered and on the tenth month, another surge of anger from the political incompetence and corruption of the Gambian system made me leave that country, and back to Motherland; "The world 9ja" (Nigeria) with again, a barely seven-month-old boy in my hands with two baby colts, jeez! That was real mental madness ladies and gentle men! Put yourself in my shoes briefly and feel my joy and pains under such circumstance… It was real madness; crazy adventures! It is such a long story and has no relevance to this book, particularly.

For two years in Nigeria, I battled with the highest level of corruption, total lack of patriotism, cheating, betrayals and near political and social chaos. I was once more embittered, enraged for the damages being daily meted out to my beloved country by: political, social, economical, industrial and academic sectors. Most of the times, I do shed tears for those damages done to my beloved country and citizens but, the feeling of impotency will usually overwhelm and again, the only option will be to take my treasured family and go (the only thing of valued I ever owned) leaving every other thing behind me; this time I moved once again to Ghana from Nigeria.

On arrival in Ghana, as usual, I must have to find new accommodation, new schools for the kids, new language and culture to learn; new friends to make and new diets to incorporate. Frankly, it had never being an easy task with children under your care to engage in such moves. The effect of all those forced moves on my children will be ascertained in their later years of adulthood. My children were unable to master any one language as a result of those continuous moves but, however, they still managed to cope and very well they did coped. They were able to keep broad smiles on their faces as they were joggled from one continent to the other in search of fair and just nations; nations with their mass population at heart prior to enacting and promulgation of laws that shall govern their citizens; Everywhere we went, people wonder, "what great children!" their respective manners of my out of these chaos are impeachable but, for me, my children were too shy and too humble to my liking. Barely two years had we stayed in Ghana and here we are once again in Italy.

While back in Italy with all my family members, in less than two months of stay, I noticed that the Italian system of government is too uncertain and unfair to both its very citizens and more to non-citizens. Yet again, I became very enraged under such negative system and influence. Consequently, Again, I started working over my next move but this time, my wife and the two grown up children were evidently tiered of these trips which are basically motivated by anger and lonely fights against a faceless system; My wife and children simply thought I should give up that inward fight and conform to the whims of our given system because, "you can't do anything to change the present system as it is, in their views".

That was the most devastating period for me; how could I continue this lonely fight without my family members; how can I keep moving without my beloved family crew? I was bemused in my chagrin due mostly to lack of my family allegiance in that very moment; this time I wanted to move but could not because my families were sick of it all. They also wanted a quiet and stable life as anyone else! I understood their reasons but couldn't help myself. I could not afford to close my eyes and pretend that all is well, I wish I could. Is that not the easiest thing to do? Is that not what we all do in order to keep keeping on – suffering and forcing some smiles and cracked and terse jokes miles away from the bottom of our hearts?

As things are, I cannot just go back to my third world nation and have a quiet and happy life without putting out a big revolutionary fight. There got to be a change to the better! I have in my stock, the written solutions for the kind of proactive and durable changes I wish to propagate all for public perusal and debate, but, how do I bring it up to the public awareness and make known my views to all and sundry?

On the other hand, I cannot really live with joy, hope and happiness in the First-World nation the way it is for now; until changes to the better is also propagated. I got the solution written as well on how best to go about it all for effective benefit to nations and citizens!

In the first world, no matter the level of my social and economic comforts, I still find my good self being daily battered and shattered with rage and anger against my volition, resulting from uncontrollable pains of injustice, negative manipulations and inhuman conspiracies common in these parts of the world.

Entrapped between the "Third and First-World nations as they are; my body is willing but my "subconscious-mind", (which is the only God I know respect and worship) refuses to accept and fully acknowledge these nations and their negative mental attitudes towards the simple ways of the things of creation and disrupt of simple human conveniences.

My questions therefore are: who am I? Where do I belong to? Where is the second world? Maybe the true answer to these questions may help me to live and accept the Second-World nations if I know where to find them! Worst of all, as an individual entity, I have got much to offer to our world which I so much admire and cherish. But, unfortunately, I find myself still endlessly searching for a fertile and an arable soil or better put - "the promised land" onto which I could sow my seeds for maximum yield and ingathering.

I know I am not alone in my predicament. Many are in my shoes and can easily tell outright where it hurts because they feel it and bear it. The daily and constant pains and anger which seems to find no remedy – what will be the lasting solution? Because a shot-cut solution is not a sincere and an honest solution to problems; therefore, things done without a long-term plan do flicker in a twinkle and we shall be back from wherever we started. For this reason, I ask for a lasting solution with the only feasible method I was inspired with years back; and that is- to select some children from the ages of four to six (4-6) year old boys and girls from each of the thirty-six states that make up the federal republic of Nigeria. The selected children shall be educated in a special institution: '**National Institute for Peace and Harmony'** where they will live and learn the correct leadership principles for peace and harmony to foster. In addition, those children shall learn the importance of living and applying the **'Golden Rules of Creation'** in all their respective fields of endeavor throughout their lives. This approach is for me, the only viable pathway to start honest and proactive changes in our national policies and citizenry perception towards the possible best! The past and present governing bodies in Nigeria failed to live up to the expectations of themselves, their nation and citizens; unfortunately.

Like devouring vultures, Nigeria government from inception had been busy pursuing worthless shady policies in place of invaluable, transparent and binding outreach to unite her humble citizens; *shadow is an illusion of reality therefore, cannot make real things happen.* From pursing shadow with all your might and vigor, you had knowingly or unknowingly be dishing out too much sadness to your children in the place of happiness; too much cause for hatred in place of love; too much confusion instead of comprehension. Too much cause for discord instead of harmony. Too much hopelessness instead of hopefulness and too much negativity instead of positivity! Let us therefore voluntarily incorporate the above offer or suggestion to begin a new facelift in our collective national interest for all citizens of Nigeria and neighboring countries.

Currency Up and Downgrading – *wicked global elite conspiracy*

It is questionable that in a wide wild world like ours, with as many currencies as countries making up the global communities, there exist just few currencies which enjoy full global recognition; that have got worth and value; which are serving as the real legal tenders for all nations. For example: Pound Sterling, Euro, Dollars. These are the currencies which have been and still in use and accepted as the global legal tenders for everyone to use nearly in all international and inter-continental transactions. The rest of the currencies from the other part of the world are valueless and treated as such everywhere outside their respective home territories and even within. Why should that be so?

Are you able to quantify for example, the level of damages such policies continue to inflict on other countries and mostly on the growing youth of this awesome generation?

The high value deliberately placed on certain currencies denominated as: Dollars, Euros and the Pound-Sterling is obviously encouraging and forcing a good number of people from the other parts of the world continue to flock into the cities of Europe and America, generation after generation in order to get hold of those high valued currencies so as to give them quicker leverage over their country's impoverished moneys. It is for those particular economic advantages which continue to instigate majority of the immigration and emigration issues negatively pervading Europe and American continents for decades. The majority of our global youth tend to abandon their ancestral homes in exodus to the tantalizing cities of the advanced nations of this wide-wild-world leaving behind them their loved families and cherished customs in the vain pursuit of the high-valued-first-world-currencies.´

Sorry to say this, but, let it be made clear that, those kinds of policies based on inequality and political imbalance are some of the premeditated ensemble with aim to suppress, manipulate and dominate Africa and Asian continents in a blatant show of power and prowess.

In a similar way, the national passports from other countries outside Europe and America are undervalued in their relationship. The currencies from the third-world nations – Africa, Asia and South America- have no equal values to those of the first world nations – Europe and North America- because if they do, if so be the case, that might crumble the first world economic powers which will reduce their global power and strength over the other nations. I can understand that though – the natural resources of the first world nations are slightly less and inferior to those of the third world nations. All these other global policies that encourage in-equality, segregation, suppression and exploitation help to give credence, false-power and false-superiority to the first-world nations; it is quite obvious. Isn't it?

There should be a mutual global agreement to amend those archaic laws in such a way that no nation or people be victimized, none suffers the pain and pang of injustice – to inflict pains to your neighbors is a negative feeling and also demonstrates acts of immaturity and fear. Our world is not created with the spirit of fear and faithlessness, but of strength, hope and faithfulness. Let's share everything mutually! We are brothers and sisters living in one world as one human species. I believe, after all said and done, that we should share our natural and technological resources in such a way as to benefit all humans irrespective of race or geographical location or demarcation. "United we stand and firmly; but divided we fall down apart and shatter".

The Second World - *where is it located?*

Speaking and reasoning logically, the big question to ask at this stage will be: If the technologically advanced countries are being referred to and classified as "The-First-World nations" and then, the less technologically advanced nations classified and referred to as the "Third-World-nations", where then is and who make up the "Second-World-Nations"?

On behalf of the youth from all parts of the world, I must admit through this medium to state that, it beats my sane imagination how our cherished and dearest parents, our fathers who are supposed to be watching over us with our best interests uppermost in their minds; have evidently refused to address and embrace those vital issues and challenges which disrupt global or national unity, peace and harmony as results of political immaturities and archaic laws allowed to be governing our global community. Evidently those issues are considered minor in our political agendas but, however they constitute innumerable disruption of unity, peace and harmony in every of our past or present national to global governmental discourse.

Due to all the obvious factors of global: inequality, political imbalance and injustice felt by the Less Technologically advanced countries referred to as 'Third World Nations' their youth ceaselessly risk their lives to embark on venturing into the First World Countries' in order to become "somebody" according to their erroneous beliefs.

When these children struggle against all means to arrive in the technologically advanced nations, they usually shall begin with confronting: Constant racial clashes, intolerance and xenophobia on increasing dimension; drug addiction and trafficking, rape and prostitution are all very common social hazards related directly or indirectly to the negative effects of those archaic laws which we allow to continue to dictate our collective future. Most of today's youth are angry and confused which tend to make them resort to all sorts of uncanny crimes they always justify with the insensitivity evidently shown by the governing bodies over their plight and yearnings for self-recognition – either way, such negative circumstances form part of our human lifestyle…trailing on the wrong pathway of life!

However, time is overdue for us to sincerely address those elements of disunity and disharmony pervading our national system. Fairly and sincerely addressing such negative elements will help to reduce or at least prevent most of this current and unforeseen dilemma challenging our growing youth and pushing them towards catastrophic behaviors and exodus.

We all know, believe and accept that "prevention is better than cure". Instead of spending millions of hard earned money plus our able man-power to patrol our seas chasing for illegal immigrants, drug, human and arms traffickers etcetera; and sending our adolescents to wars to kill and be killed. Why not instead make laws to mitigate or rather totally eradicate the causes from the main sources? Is prevention not better anymore than cure? When had that ceased to be so?

(Excerpt from my book- "Universal child")

MARRIAGE PROCEDURE IN UGBELLE-BIAFRA

Three days had elapsed since after Nkem's visit to the Lawrence family. After their consultation, she assumed she could go on to start dealing with the preliminary arrangements in order to be able to officially propose a marriage relationship between the two families, which would go in accord with the customs and traditions of the Ugbelle people.

In Ugbelle, for any marriage relationship to be valid and honored:

(1) Two persons will not be allowed or honored to marry and have sexual intercourse with each other if there is any trace of blood relation with the intended partner.

(2) Somehow the elders of both engaging kindred have to be informed, pampered, and entertained.

(3) The boy must pay a dowry and other material requirements for taking their beloved daughter away from her kinsmen and women. Within this phase, they take their time haggling and bargaining to get the maximum from the boy before he finally gives in and carries away their lovely daughter from them; at least, these are the good impressions to sustain the culture and traditions.

4) The real tradition is that whenever a boy meets with a girl and truly feels that he loves her and would be glad to contract a marriage relationship with her, the boy would first, at his own convenience, bring the news to the knowledge of his own family, especially to his parents. Alerted, the boy's parents' on their own personal initiative will have to seek and hire a third person (known in Ibo language as "Onye-ndu"). This person's duty is to dig for the history and background of the girl in question to find out if there has being a history of hereditary sicknesses; if the girl is clean, genuine, and

well behaved; and if she is or not an out-caste "Osu" or possessed by devilish spirit "Ogbanje" and so many other things, even though they are all based more or less on superstitions. The parents' of the girl on their side could choose or not to set up a similar investigation against the boy and his background. These usually take a couple of days. Also, it is the duty of the Onye-ndu to carry over any form of message from either party before, within, or after the immediate matrimonial nagotiations and haggling.

 (5) Assuming the boy's family is satisfied with the result of the investigations--after all convictions and a decision is arrived at to marry the proposed girl in question, they will promptly deliver a message through the Onye-ndu to the family of the girl notifying them that on a fixed date, they are coming to pay them a marriage-proposal visit. Being formally informed, the girl's family will have to make a response through the same medium back to the family of the boy, accepting or rejecting their request.

If accepted, the reply will read that they will be waiting for them on the appointed date. These visits are usually made accompanied by ten liters of palm wine (in a calabash) and few bottles of wines and spirits, maybe, other things also. Basically, palm wine is the traditional alcoholic drink of the people for occasions like this. This must always be followed with few big and healthy nuts of Kola. Note that, at this initial stage of courtesy or courtship, the boy and the girl may or may not be present during those visits of notification of marriage interest and responses. This is usually carried out between the "Onye-ndu" and selected willing elders and closest relations. The scene is always festive.

(6) All having been said and done, the day arrives for the big feast--paying of the dowry and whisking the girl away from her parents and kinsmen, women, and friends to start a new life in a new home with a new surname. On that appointed date and time, the boy, elegantly dressed, arrives at the girl's family house accompanied by his whole

contingent: father, mother, both grannies, and almost all the kinsmen, women, and children willing to feast and party. They carry along with them their own prepared food and drinks apart from those things traditionally demanded by the peoples' customs for a marriage contract. The place will be ready with seats, tables, music, and microphones with a Master of the Ceremony--MC--that will coordinate and see to the smooth running of the occasion. They will sit waiting in the crowded town hall with all their things, talking and laughing in lower voices while the local high-life music infiltrates the hall and its surroundings with a familiar rhythm from Osita Osadebe, Oliver de Coque, Oriental Brothers and so many others.

Some people prefer to sit outside in the open air under orange and mango trees with their seats and tables, mostly those who have nothing to add to the occasion except for their attendance, which is highly valued and welcomed.

A marriage ceremony in Ugbelle is generally regarded by the people as a moment of joy and jubilation--particularly by the mothers. That they had been able to bring up a child to the age of marriage who found the love of her/his heart is seen as a huge stepping stone to becoming independent. The mothers usually are happy for the success of their children, wishing them well in their secret prayers. There is no sense of hurry in these marriage occasions. The general attitude of the girls' parents is that they want to be pampered before they give away their beloved daughter. It does not matter how long it will take. As the visitors sit for nearly an hour waiting, the girl's kinsmen and women start to arrive and appear from different corners one after the other, a pretence of reluctance written all over their faces--nothing personal! It's all part and parcel of the ceremony.

The special day arrived for Christiana and Louis. The hall filled with both hosts and visitors. The boy's father, Mr. Louis Obison, stood up and requested silence; this was granted, and he began:

First he introduced himself as the man behind the marriage activities, the backbone whose duty it was to make this a success. He introduced his son, his contingent, and of course, the main purpose of the visit, which all were already well aware of. Before concluding, he handed over all their presents that were comprised of several calabashes of palm wine, liquor, and spirits. As he finished, he sat down and handed over the audience to the MC. The MC is a man who knows the culture very well and does all possible for things to move on according to the rules and regulations. He introduced the parents of the girl to the visitors and handed over the microphone to Mr. Lawrence, as the head of the family and the reason for everyone gathered there today. Taking the microphone in his left hand, Mr. Lawrence extended the right to lift a tray full of the mixture of creamy and pink cola nuts. Before he could ask, everyone was already on their feet because they understood the rules--time for prayers, thanksgiving, and official opening of the occasion. As they stood ready, he began thanking the ancestors for their guidance and protection against all evils, and for all visitors to find their respective way back to their homes and wherever they came from at the end of the occasion. Thanking God also for everything in their lives, he finished, handed over the tray of cola nuts to the MC, and sat down. The MC respectfully carried the nuts to the eldest man in the hall from the host's side, Mr. Amos Awu, who thanked the gods and ancestors of their land of everything and who then quickly blessed the cola nuts. Then the tedious task of breaking them into smaller pieces began so that everyone would have a share of it. This first act symbolized that all is well and you are welcome to our house.

Phase 1-The custom is that after they complete the breaking of the cola nuts, the younger boys and girls present by custom volunteered to carry and distribute the nuts to everyone in and out of the hall. The custom is that as the cola distributors present to your seat, you take your time to select the piece of your choice while feigning courtesy and gratitude. From this stage, everything moves faster also because, every indigenous of Ugbelle is well aware of the phases and steps of the entire marriage procedure.

Phase 2- Before concluding sharing of the nuts, the most senior man from the visitors will have to stand up and walk straight to the high table where all the jars and calabashes of palm wine drinks for the occasion are waiting. A cup will be offered to him by the host; he will then chose from the calabashes and fill his cup with the white palm wine, and pour a customary libation to the gods and ancestors believed to be invisibly present among the living, especially in big ceremonies like traditional marriages. After each drop of wine on the floor in front of him, some prayers of thanksgiving and gratitude will be offered to the ancestors for watching well over us. In fact, every word uttered then will usually be followed by a drop of wine. When he finishes praying and blessing the occasion, he will quickly gulp down the rest of the wine in the same cup, and with that, mark the opening of the floor and freedom for all to start drinking and dancing while the rest of the background activities will quietly go on. This allows some minutes for everyone to get a bit of the drinks before the most apprehensive--

Phase 3- is the time for the marriage to be officially confirmed or nullified depending on the next action of the girl. As the bride and reason for this August gathering, she will have to demonstrate to everyone that she has accepted willingly to marry the boy in question and that after this ceremony, she will follow this boy back to his home.

 How do we show that? The father of the girl or his representative will have to pour a cup of the palm wine, fish the girl out from the crowd, and hand over the cup of wine to her. Then something happens in most traditional marriages in Ugbelle, and also in many parts of Nigeria as a whole, that is similar to when the Catholic priest declares husband and wife with the sign of a kiss and the offering of the marriage ring as a bond binding them both officially together for the better and for the worst. The father or his representative will tell the girl, "Here, my beloved daughter; you know why all these people are here today, take a sip, or a kiss of this wine, carry the rest to the man of your heart in these multitude of people gathered here today." This is a very serious moment; there is absolute silence, all eyes, over five to ten thousand pairs of eyes, are on this young adolescent girl (most times, this will be the very first time the girl will have the privilege to taste an alcoholic drink). Some became so shy at this stage that they will be unable to continue with the demands of the ceremony, and that marriage bond will come to a sad ending because the girl was unable to go on with all those steps.

The game is such that, at this stage, they will sit the boy somewhere in the crowd, maybe the second or third row of the seats so that the whole thing does not seem easy. Sometimes also to dramatize the occasion, the girl pretends not to see the boy and continues to walk among the midst of the crowd feigning a search for her lover. When she wants to ease the tensions among the crowd, she will walk straight to her lover with the cup of wine. Getting in front of him, she will stop and kneel down while offering the cup of wine. As soon as the boy receives that wine and takes a sip of it, there will be an instant uproar among the crowd, symbolizing a great success for their journey and efforts. The music will come louder, the real dancing, drinking, and feasting takes off at this stage in earnest because the mission have been accomplished and successful!

Many marriage proposals have ended up at that stage. When the girl hand-over the cup of wine to the boy, her job is then done with. The occasion is declared open for all, and she will then get up immediately and disappear from the crowd; though she may rejoin them later for the dancing and feasting. With that, we move to

Phase 4-It is now certain beyond reasonable doubt that the girl has accepted to love, marry, and live with the boy. As custom demands, before or after the end of the feasting and dancing, the visitors will be ready to go back to their own community together with their new wife. They have conquered! However, there remains the final confirmation to be done by the girl before it will all be over. The motive for this trip was meant for the girl to really get to familiarize herself with the direct family members of the boy. She should by law stay with the boy and family for a minimum of four days and a maximum of eight on this trip. She has to be doubly sure she can live with and be able to support for long the boy and family. She has to feel the people and judge them from her own point of view. After eight days has elapsed, and she finally confirms to her parents that she can handle it, she is going to be able to cope, the marriage will be sealed. Divorce is very rare in Ugbelle, that is why you are allowed time to decide and to make up your mind before going in, once in, getting out is tedious. On the eighth day, the boy and maybe with one or two friends will have to take the girl back to her family one final time, with just a calabash of palm wine as stipulated by tradition. At the volition of the boy, he may want to make other presents to the wife-to-be such as jewelry, dresses, shoes, or liquid-cash. On arriving at the girl's parents,' the boy complies by handing back the girl to the parents in better shape than when he whisked her away from them eight days ago. After handing over the girl and the calabash of wine, the boy and his friends will leave and allow the family some time to listen to the girl's experiences of the boy's family, village, and of the boy in particular. Once she confirms this last time that she wants go on and marry the Nigger-raw, that then takes us direct to

Phase 5-After a minimum of two days and a maximum of four from the day the girl was brought back by the husband-to-be, tradition demands that the girl should also return the last calabash with which she was accompanied back home. The return of that particular calabash by the girl simply means that "Yes" old boy, I have decided to marry you after all at all cost, so let's get down to business!" Because, even at this stage, the girl still have the right not to continue with the marriage. In such rare cases, the calabash shall not be returned by the girl but by the Onye-ndu" or the calabash will never be sent back. Which will also deliver its bitter but simple message, "Boy, I am sorry; I couldn't help it; you can try your luck somewhere else, sorry." That is the end to that particular marriage move and courtesy. As she instead returned the calabash, immediately we move into the next stage,

Phase 6-Returning of the calabash by the girl, carries with the gesture such messages as: All plans should proceed according to the tradition and custom of the people. Every previous plan in regard to the marriage should go on. At this stage, once again, the services of the intermediary--Onye-ndu--will be required to send across a word to the girl's family notifying them of their intention to come on a given date to conclude the rest of the conditions in order to legally take the girl home forever and start a normal family as husband and wife.

This stage is known as "Igba nmaya nwanyi or "Ime ego isi nwanyi," meaning the paying of the dowry over the girl. Nothing can stop the marriage at this stage except the girl alone. The paying of the dowry is a very romantic business initiated by the girl's parents to demonstrate to the visitors how much they cherish and love their baby girl and are not willing to give her away for nothing. There will be much haggling between both parents without the prospective couple . . . there will be drinks and booze like the first time but with less tension. When the hagglers of the dowry have finally finished, and a mutual agreement arrived at, the girl shall only then legally becomes the boy's wife. With that, they have been granted the inalienable right and license to marry, tango, make love and procreate!

Now we go back to our couple, Christy and Louis. All was said and done with Phase 6, and six months later, Christy conceived. In another nine months, she gave birth to a bouncing baby boy whom they later named Amaechi Obi!